D0322711

Lucy Brown has made television programmes around the world for the BBC, ITV, Channel 4, Nickelodeon and Disney. She has TV credits on BAFTA and RTS award-winning children's programmes and the acclaimed flagship architecture series *Grand Designs*. Lucy is Principal Lecturer and Head of Film and Television at the University of Greenwich. She is a fellow of the Higher Education Academy, winner of a Vice-Chancellor's Award for Excellence in International Engagement and a regular juror at international media festivals.

Lyndsay Duthie is an award-winning executive producer with television credits for ITV, BBC, Channel 4, Channel 5 and Sky. Her career has included ten years originating and producing hit series at ITV, as well as running her own company, Ice Blue Media. Lyndsay is Principal Lecturer and Course Director for the University of Hertfordshire's Film & TV Programme. She is a fellow of the Higher Education Academy, winner of the Vice-Chancellor's Award for Excellence in Education and Graduate Success, and has judged at the Royal Television Society Awards (RTS) and International Emmys.

'By capturing the modern, global world of television production from the mouths of those involved in some of the industry's biggest shows, *The TV Studio Production Handbook* [opens] a window on the real world of programme-making alongside the theory.'
  – David Williams, BBC Creative Director of Entertainment North

'This book, written by two women who have triumphed in the trenches of TV production, gives you the tools you need to negotiate today's rapidly evolving international TV landscape.'
  – Shelly Goldstein, TV writer-producer-comedy consultant to ABC, CBS, Fox, NBC, Sony

'A comprehensive and useful guide for those taking their first steps in the TV industry.'
  – Emily Gale, Head of Talent, FremantleMedia UK

THE
TV
STUDIO
PRODUCTION
HANDBOOK

LUCY BROWN AND LYNDSAY DUTHIE

LIS - LIBRARY

Date	Fund
20/10/20	T

Order No.

02491032

University of Chester

BLOOMSBURY ACADEMIC

LONDON · NEW YORK · OXFORD · NEW DELHI · SYDNEY

BLOOMSBURY ACADEMIC
Bloomsbury Publishing Plc
50 Bedford Square, London, WC1B 3DP, UK
1385 Broadway, New York, NY 10018, USA

BLOOMSBURY, BLOOMSBURY ACADEMIC and the Diana logo are trademarks of
Bloomsbury Publishing Plc

First published in Great Britain 2016 by. I.B. Tauris & Co. Ltd.
Reprinted by Bloomsbury Academic 2019

Copyright © Ice Blue Media Ltd and Lucy Brown, 2016

Ice Blue Media Ltd and Lucy Brown have asserted their rights under the
Copyright, Designs and Patents Act, 1988, to be identified as Author of this work.

For legal purposes the Acknowledgements on p. ix constitute an extension
of this copyright page.

All rights reserved. No part of this publication may be reproduced or transmitted
in any form or by any means, electronic or mechanical, including photocopying,
recording, or any information storage or retrieval system, without prior
permission in writing from the publishers.

Bloomsbury Publishing Plc does not have any control over, or responsibility for,
any third-party websites referred to or in this book. All internet addresses given
in this book were correct at the time of going to press. The author and publisher
regret any inconvenience caused if addresses have changed or sites have ceased
to exist, but can accept no responsibility for any such changes.

A catalogue record for this book is available from the British Library.

A catalog record for this book is available from the Library of Congress.

ISBN: PB: 978-1-3501-4407-1
ePDF: 978-1-7867-3041-1
eBook: 978-1-7867-2041-2

Typeset by Out of House Publishing
Printed and bound in Great Britain

To find out more about our authors and books visit www.bloomsbury.com
and sign up for our newsletters.

To our boys

Elijah, Rudy and Zach

Contents

Images

Images 2, 3 and 4 are the authors' own.

Acknowledgements

Thank you to everyone who has helped with the making of this book. To our families for their continued support, love and encouragement and to everyone we interviewed for kindly taking the time to speak to us and share their wisdom. We thank each and every one of you: Lisa Armstrong, Dom Bird, Posy Brewer, Kate Broadhurst, Lyn Burgess, Rupert Carey, Maddy Darrall, Nigel Duthie, Emily Gale, Campbell Glennie, Shelly Goldstein, Richard Holloway, Katherine Morgan, David Nugent, Simon Paintin, Andrew Parker, James Penfold, Job Rabkin, Simon Reay, Derek Richards, Kieran Roberts, Sam Snape, Martin Scott, Graham Sherrington, Adrian Swift, Neil Thompson, Werner Walian, Yan Wang, Karl Warner, Andy Waters, Matthew Welch, Jet Wilkinson, David Williams, James Winter and Rebecca Yang.

It has been a great pleasure to speak to so many talented people, and travel to Australia, the USA, China and across the UK to do so. We also thank Isabelle Rawlings for transcribing the interviews!

Thanks to the University of Hertfordshire and the University of Greenwich – and to Judy Glasman, Peter Richardson, Steven Adams, Gregory Sporton and Stephen Kennedy for supporting us. We would also like to thank all of our colleagues and students who have inspired us to write this book, and Kim Akass for introducing us to our wonderful publishers I.B.Tauris. Special thanks to our editor Philippa Brewster for guiding us through this exciting journey.

This book has evolved out of the many years we have worked in the TV industry, and we would like to thank all the inspiring people we have met and worked with along the way who have contributed to our knowledge.

We hope you have found this book useful and look forward to hearing all about your productions via our facebook page https://www.facebook.com/TVStudioProductionHandbook or tweet us at @lucyaabrown and @Lyndsayduthie.

PART ONE

Standby!

1

INTRODUCTION

Welcome to the definitive guide to making studio productions. This book is packed full of live case studies, tips, jargon, real-world scripts and exclusive interviews with directors, producers and top TV executives, working in the industry in the UK, USA, Australia and China, to ensure you get off to a flying start.

Having worked in the industry for twenty years, we have honed our craft as programme-makers working for broadcasters such as BBC, ITV, Channel 4, Sky and Nickelodeon and now, as media educators, we share our knowledge and passion for TV with the next generation of programme-makers. While a lot of our students arrive with some knowledge of how to make a film, the studio environment still holds an element of mystery. This book is a practical guide, providing you with invaluable insider knowledge.

Do you really know the protocol of a working gallery? Do you know the countdown procedure? What 'falling off air' means? Well you soon will!

We have tried to make this book as conversational as possible with many references to television shows you will know to bring our words to life. Watch the shows, follow the book and make your own versions. The more shows you make, the better you get!

Part one of the book gives you everything to get started, beginning with the big idea. Why are some ideas more successful than others? How do you come up with an idea? How does a programme get commissioned? What do you need to create a pilot to sell your idea? All of these are key questions with answers from top programme-makers from around the world.

Then we move on to pre-production planning – all the elements of production management and the various paperwork that is essential to complete for a smooth-running production. We have included templates for budgeting, scheduling and call sheets. We have also looked at how to develop your idea for television. Each chapter includes exercises and top tips to summarise our points for each stage of production.

Part two of the book looks more in-depth at the different genres that you find in the studio. From drama, news, children's and food, to game shows and prime-time talent and reality shows, we have it all covered. In each chapter we look at a very brief history of each genre – this is not definitive (this is a practical book) but more to give you a flavour of some of the key turning points that relate to that genre. From our unique access to the television industry we have packed these chapters with exclusive interviews from the world's leading industry experts, such as executive producers of *Weakest Link*, *The Voice* and *China's Next Top Model*, directors of *Neighbours* and *Top Gear*, a commissioning editor of *Channel 4 News* and a producer of *The Middle*. We have used live case studies of the biggest global brands, including script extracts from *Coronation Street*, *Britain's Got Talent*, *Big Brother*, *Teletubbies*, *Saturday Kitchen* and *The Chase* for you to block through in your workshops – before devising your own versions.

To pull this all together as an *aide-mémoire* we have devised our own S.T.U.D.I.O. checklist, which is relevant for every single studio production. If you follow this you will be on the road to success.

S.T.U.D.I.O. Toolkit

S – Set up

There is a lot of prep done before the crew and production team even arrive at the studio. The director and producer spend hours breaking the script down and working out how to bring the script to life in the studio. The producer needs to make sure all the logistics are handled and the director needs to work out how many cameras to use and if the show has a presenter, which camera they will talk to and when.

The studio set has to be created: it is just an empty shell until the producer and director communicate their vision to the art team who can then start to work their magic – constructing, building, painting and creating the set.

Do not underestimate how long it takes to set up in the studio. Studio productions often involve large crews, with lots of equipment to get ready. Schedule this time carefully so you are not up against it from the word go. Allowing enough rehearsal time is paramount to the success of a good studio TV production, and this is even more crucial for live productions. Preparation, preparation, preparation. Studio filming days are typically long (10 to 12 hours a day). They may start at seven o'clock in the morning with a production meeting and tech check (technical inspection of the equipment) and not wrap (the industry term for the end of filming) until seven o'clock in the evening. Further details of how a typical studio day is broken down and an example of a schedule can be found in Chapter 5.

Rehearsal time should be built-in to the set-up time. There are three key stages of the rehearsal process in a studio production, and these stages are often referred to as the block-through, the stagger-through and the run-through. The block-through stage provides invaluable time to work out camera angles and moves with the crew, and mark locations for presenters, actors or contributors. The director is typically on the studio floor during the block-through – discussing shots with the camera operators. Studio productions can be single-camera set-ups, more common in drama, or multiple-camera set-ups, with cameras going into double figures for some big-budget prime-time studio shows. You should never underestimate the value of doing an extensive block-through as Simon Reay, Emmy-nominated director of photography (DOP) of drama, factual and commercials says:

> As soon as that camera gets put up it all becomes about the camera and the later that happens, in my mind, the better! It's all about the performers in their space and that's what's important – certainly everything I've ever done, you don't need the camera on so early, leave it and leave it and leave it. Let the artists do what they want to do and that should then inform where your camera goes.

Stage two is the stagger-through – in which, as the name suggests, there is a lot of stopping and starting while presenters/actors go over the script and camera operators adjust their positions. Positions are often marked on the studio floor with gaffer tape to help this process. The director is typically in the gallery at this point and communicates instructions to the camera operators over a talkback system. Meanwhile the floor manager (FM), or first assistant director (AD, in drama), is in charge of everything running smoothly on the studio floor. The FM/AD ensures all talent/actors/contributors know where they need to be and all props are in the right place.

The final rehearsal stage is the run-through. This is the last opportunity to make sure everyone knows what they are doing and the show is the correct length. During this stage the action is played out, without any stops. The gallery production assistant (PA), sometimes known as a script supervisor, is responsible for timings. Any necessary changes required to ensure the show comes in at the correct length are made at the end of the run-through and revisions made to the script. To become a PA you need to be confident and organised, as Katherine Morgan, a live gallery PA with credits on *Match of the Day*, *Mastermind* and *A Question of Sport* advises:

> You need to remain calm in stressful situations, especially when working in 'live' TV, as things change at the last minute and you need to be able to react quickly and with confidence to relay changes over talkback so everyone knows where they are on the script, what's next and how long is left on each item and on the overall duration.

All shows are given a running time and overrunning is not an option! For a pre-recorded show this is easier to manage as the show is not live and any additional material can be cut out and mistakes re-shot as 'pick ups' at the end of the show. But, as they say in show business, 'time is money' and no one wants to overrun on a studio day as this can be hugely costly for any crew with overtime in their contracts! For a live show there is the risk of 'falling off air', meaning when a show is cut before it wraps up naturally, for example the presenter is mid-sentence and they cut to the ad break. This looks unprofessional and should be avoided at all costs.

This is why, on live award shows such as the Oscars or the British Academy of Film and Television Arts (BAFTAs), everyone nominated is briefed before the show, so that they know how long they have to say their 'thank you's' and are strategically placed by the producer for easy access to the stage to avoid long walks that eat into valuable production time.

Every programme has a timeslot and running time, these are arranged in advance by the channel and cannot be messed with. The only real exceptions are big breaking news stories of national importance and popular live sports events such as Wimbledon or the World Cup you will have noticed that during long sets or a penalty shoot-out, the presenter and/or screen text apologise for the delay to the normal running of the schedule due to the overrunning of the game/breaking news story and content may be moved to a sister channel.

So to set up you need to know the length of your show, allow enough rehearsal time and importantly don't overrun!

T – Talent

What do we mean by talent? In TV terms talent refers to the presenter of a factual or entertainment programme, the news anchor, or actor in a sitcom or soap opera. They are often the best-paid member of the studio production especially if they are a known name!

Attaching a big international name to a series (like Piers Morgan, Kylie Minogue or actors Woody Harrelson or Jennifer Aniston) can help to secure a commission, but this has to be budgeted for as Rebecca Yang, CEO of IPCN, distributor of international brands *The Voice of China* and *China's Got Talent* says of the Chinese TV market: 'Celebrity names now account for more than two thirds of the budget in most of the shows, it has gone crazy.'

Talent is one of the most important ingredients for a successful show of any genre. The casting process is key to finding the right talent for your show. Everyone that appears on the show has to gel – your actors or co-presenters need to get on and have on-screen chemistry. This process can take time with auditions and screen tests, and the channel often requiring final approval. Large shows have dedicated casting teams led by a casting producer. Hiring a celebrity can be crucial to the success of a show. Adrian Swift, executive producer of *The Voice Australia* and Head of Content, Production and Development, Nine Network Australia says: 'celebrities get people in the front door – as in it gets your show noticed and creates a lot of publicity for your show and that brings with it an audience.'

Talent is chosen to match broadcasters' brand values. Each channel thinks very carefully about who they want to represent their channel – are they a good fit for the channel brand, have they got what it takes to be the face of the channel? We know what to expect when we see certain names attached to a programme and as such celebrities often work exclusively for a channel – Simon Cowell in the UK airs his shows on ITV, Ant and Dec are the face of ITV entertainment, winners of multiple Royal Television Society (RTS) and BAFTAs for shows such as *I'm a Celebrity… Get Me Out of Here*, *Ant & Dec's Saturday Night Takeaway* and *Britain's Got Talent*. The audience know what to expect – they are cheeky chappies, likeable and fun, whereas Simon Cowell and Piers Morgan have built hugely successful careers playing the 'villain' prepared to speak their minds, even if it means upsetting the contributors and the audience. This can become a talking point, referred to as water-cooler TV.

The audience always has to be in mind when you choose your talent. If it's a young skewed show you will need to get the right 'type' and this will be very different from someone required for a Saturday prime-time family audience.

Dealing with talent, especially big names, can be tricky. Most producers and directors will have stories to tell you of their run-ins with difficult actors and presenters. In Chapter 5 we will tell you ways to deal with this and avoid potential pitfalls.

U – Unity

For a successful show you need a united front. There are many departments all working together that all need to have a shared vision.

Studio productions rely on teamwork and everyone has an essential role to play, in front of and behind the screens – from the runner, the most junior member of the production team, to the executive producer. Production teams vary in size from as little as five on a small, low-budget show to hundreds for big brands and films. Whatever the size of the production team it is important to have unity and everyone pulling in the same direction and working for the good of the show and to make the best show possible.

So who are all these people that work on a TV show? The production team is broadly split into the 'organisers' – consisting of a production manager, production co-ordinator and production secretary – who will be in charge of the logistics, ordering transport for the key talent to get to the studio and booking any required accommodation. Call sheets will be sent out so that everyone knows exactly what time to arrive on set and how to get there.

The other half of the production team can be referred to as the 'editorial and creative' team and are in charge of the content of the show – what is actually said/done on-screen. Typically, this includes the executive producer, producer, director, assistant producers, researchers and scriptwriters.

In most cases people working in television are freelancers and the production team typically have longer job contracts, as they are hired for the pre-production process. The technical team members are referred to as the 'crew' and are typically hired for shorter periods that allow them enough time to do their key studio roles (floor manager, camera, sound, art department, costume, post-production). The crew consists of a team of people who prep the set and equipment and enhance the technical look of the show. The art department (under the art director) will ensure the design of the set, and make-up and costume will ensure that the talent and contributors look and are dressed the part.

With so many departments and people working on a typical show, you can see how important it is to know your role and understand the role of everyone else to ensure the smooth running of the studio production. We'll look at studio production roles in full detail in Chapter 4 so that you hit the floor running and begin to get an understanding of the career route you would like to follow.

It is important to get the right crew for the job. Often a director and producer hire the same people as they know they are a 'safe pair of hands' and have proved their worth on previous gigs. This is why networking in the TV industry is so important. You have to meet the right people, but not just that, once you are given your opportunity, you have to impress and keep impressing to get hired again. There is a saying in the TV industry that 'you are only as good as your last job'. It's a very small world and because teamwork is so important, people want to hire those who have a good reputation at doing the best job possible but are also good to spend time with and won't be moody or unhelpful. The hours are long and you often have to go away for periods of time so being likeable, professional and good at your job is important. Maddy Darrall, company director of Darrall Macqueen and executive producer of *Teletubbies* and *Topsy and Tim* has these words of wisdom:

> Make sure you work with people who are really good team players, because working on any studio production is intense. They are long days, and it is a large portion of your life and you have got to work with people that you are compatible with on both a creative and a personal level ... the team has got to be right ... it is all about the team, off-screen and on-screen.

So how can you avoid conflict and remain professional at all times in such a difficult and fast-paced environment? Here are five key points to remember that will help you get noticed and help you to get your next studio production gig!

1. Don't play on your phone or fall asleep on the job! It sounds crazy but we've seen runners trying to catch 40 winks! Making excuses about the long days won't wash – you'll either lose your job on the spot or won't get rehired.
2. Do be a team player – ready to pitch in and help out. Ask yourself, 'what more can I do?'
3. Do arrive early and make sure you have read your call sheet.
4. Do be friendly and enthusiastic – no one wants to spend time with someone who is negative or grumpy.
5. Don't be afraid to ask for assistance or guidance. It's much better for everyone that you get a job done the first time round rather than waiting until it is too late and everyone is stressed by mistakes.

D – Director

The director's role is all about communication, fast decision-making and a clear vision. A studio TV director oversees the creative elements of a production and guides the crew and on-screen talent. The director is typically brought on board after the producer and, depending on the genre of the show, can be involved from the pre-production stage through to post-production. The director must have a thorough understanding of the script and format of the show to bring the script to life. They must understand the tone and the nuances of the show and work with the crew art department, lighting, camera, sound and post-production – to communicate their vision. In the gallery, the director works very closely with the production assistant to ensure all the required material is shot to the correct duration. The director also works closely with the floor manager. The floor manager acts as the director's eye on the studio floor and there must be clear communication from the director to the studio floor via the floor manager. The director also works closely with the producer – providing technical direction in guiding set and lighting plans and costume design. The director may be involved with the producer in the casting process. It is important that the director and presenters/actors respect one another and work well together to get the required performances, so a director will often sit in with the producer on auditions and view showreels and screen tests.

Directors should be highly organised. The director needs to meticulously plan every camera shot and prepare camera cards and a shot list, perhaps working with a storyboard artist to further work out camera sizes and angles. Storyboards are particularly useful for complicated drama scenes.

During the shoot, the studio director is pivotal to the success of the show, leading the crew and talent during rehearsal and sitting in the gallery and calling every shot that they want the camera operators to make. If a shot isn't called it won't be seen on-screen! On low-budget, small shows the director will also double up as the vision mixer – cutting the show as the action happens. Most studio directors start as gallery runners and work up to be vision mixers or production assistants and then directors.

Not all studio shows are edited live or as live so the director also needs to be in the edit for the post-production stage – overseeing visual effects and sound design.

It is a challenging and competitive job, so how do you stand out from the crowd? Jet Wilkinson, a drama director of popular Australian soaps *Neighbours* and *Home and Away* has this advice:

> You have to be able to have a voice, make it your own, yet at the same time do it all on time and within the constraints of [the show] … So it's finding that balance of having your own voice within a huge machine so that you can have longevity in the work that you do.

With so much responsibility a good director needs to be creative, efficient, an excellent communicator and must be able to problem-solve and stay calm under pressure. In a studio gallery environment there is so much going on at any one time – everyone looks to the director for leadership and it's important that the director gives off confidence, knows what they are doing but importantly can relay this to the crew and talent and find solutions to any problems. Contrary to stereotypes about film and TV directors it is not a requirement to shout at or terrorise your crew. Good directors know how to get the best out of their crew and talent – they have authority by being encouraging and supportive and earning their team's respect.

I – Innovation

There is a saying that there are no new ideas, but you can give it a fresh spin. Talent shows have been broadcast on TV since the 1960s, but this genre has been reinvented with new dimensions making the most of technical advances through the use of interactive live viewer vote. Shows such as *X Factor* and *Got Talent* refreshed the brand by bringing the audience something new by showing the audition process and what happened beyond the stage and also emphasising the singers' back stories, adding a human touch to make the audience root for their favourites. With *The Voice* it was the introduction of the chairs and not being able to judge on appearances.

Every genre from drama to news to game shows has to continually think of new ways to cover the same topics to avoid predictability and maintain audience interest and viewing figures. An essential part of being on the editorial side of a TV programme, in development or as a scriptwriter, is thinking of new and exciting ways to tell familiar stories. What are the fresh angles you can bring to an already recognisable format? You have to constantly ask yourself what is unique about this idea, and what will excite the audience and the commissioning editor to get your idea commissioned and on the screen? David Williams, Creative Director of Entertainment North at the BBC explains what he looks for in a good idea:

> I suppose there are a number of factors. It is often not the idea that excites but it's the way into them that is exciting. That might be a technical innovation that tells the story, it might be a mechanic which brings it together in a different way, it might be a slight blurring of different techniques all of which give it a turn of the wheel that make it feel new and exciting. That's not to say that when a new idea first comes through the door it is not a brilliant thing, but often it is about doing what is going to deliver well to an audience when they have an appetite for an idea and delivering it in a different way.

Companies and channels are always on the lookout for the next big hit show. But remember that to come up with original content you need to know what has come before, and that means that you need to consume everything you can get your hands on – watch old episodes of soaps, comedies, quiz shows and game shows, and start thinking about how you can bring a fresh approach to something. What's the unique selling point of your idea?

O – Obstacles

Be a pessimist and think ahead. Anticipate what could go wrong and have a solution ready!

On a TV show it is typically one of the jobs of the producer to overcome obstacles. What's the worst that could happen? What do we have in place to combat that? You need back-ups for your main contributors, and sometimes even back-ups for them! What if your presenter is running late? Can we get the presenter to stay overnight to minimise that issue? Can we set up the night before?

In production it's essential to be a good problem-solver. In the world of TV things will not always go to plan, actors and contributors will fall down, your favourite camera operator might get another gig, you might not have the budget you want for all the cameras – so what are you going to do about it? You have to find solutions and quickly. You have to break down the script and work out the budget and schedule to carefully bring your idea to life.

You need a 'can do' attitude. The magic of TV throws up many dilemmas that the producer and team have to overcome, as Werner Walian, producer of the hit TV series *The Middle* says when explaining the issues he faced filming the show on the Warner Bros. studios in Hollywood when it is supposed to be set in the Midwest (quite a challenge!):

> I will have anywhere from 150 to 200 people working with me from costumes to post to art direction to location and basically it's my job when the script comes to me, to break it down and figure out. Right how are we going to be able to make this next episode within the five days that we have to shoot the show? It's very challenging for a show that takes place in Indiana but we shoot here in California. Indiana is very flat and [there are] not too many mountains, no palm trees and lots of corn and then we have to try and create a sense that when we are outside, for the location work, it looks somewhat like the Midwest so those are big challenges!

These are all things we have learnt through experience, trial and error. If you can demonstrate this kind of intuition for programme-making, you will go far.

So remember

S – set-up time – always prep
T – talent – make your programme come to life
U – unity – does everyone have a shared vision?
D – director – the creative visionary
I – innovation – don't make derivative – make defining
O – obstacles – be a troubleshooter and create solutions!

Follow these rules and you will be the kind of person the industry needs. Now read on to get your idea started...

2

THE BIG IDEA

The first stage of the development process is thinking of an idea that translates well to screen. The TV industry needs ideas, and lots of them! Ideas are very much the lifeblood of the industry, a vital part of the production process. Every single TV programme is based on an idea. Someone somewhere came up with the idea for every show that you watch: whatever the genre, whatever the platform – mobile, web, TV – it's all about the idea! Rebecca Yang has this to say:

> The way people consume content has changed, on mobile devices, on tablets, but at the end of the day, it needs to be content you want to watch; you want to see people laugh, you want to see sad stories, you want to see human connection. The content needs to matter.

If you can learn this crucial skill, to think up ideas that work wonderfully on TV and resonate with an audience, it becomes much easier to break into the television industry, get noticed and move up the ranks quickly. At every job interview you will more than likely be asked if you have an idea for a programme and it isn't enough to just have one idea, you really need to show that you are living and breathing television and have a whole host of ideas up your sleeve. It's time to put your thinking cap on and learn some of the creative idea skills to make you stand out from the crowd. In this chapter we will share what we have learnt from commissioners and top TV executives working in the industry, as well as from our own experience. We will look at some of the techniques used to help stimulate ideas and help you to create original content that TV producers and commissioners want. Sometimes good ideas can be down to timing, as Dom Bird, Head of Formats at Channel 4 points out:

> There are good ideas that have never been made because it wasn't the right moment, and quite often you just need things to align, so you need things to become relevant and something that wasn't

relevant last year or the year before, for whatever reason, becomes relevant or of the moment, which unlocks it.

So you will probably notice that there are often trends in TV content at the same time. This could be a renewed interest in sport-themed shows in the run-up to the Olympics, which in another year might not hold the same appeal. These could be global trends or specific to a key territory. Rebecca Yang talks about how social change is impacting the taste in Chinese TV programming:

> It's the demographic that you really need to cater for, it's not necessarily the platform. The demographic for online are younger, are edgier. How do you choose a young fresh host that will tailor to their taste? What are the latest trends? What is everyone talking about? You need to look at what people care about, then you go, 'a dating show would work in China!' Now the divorce rate is very high, so a marriage show would work in China. Back in the day people were only buying new flats, so there was no such thing as a renovation show but now people are buying second-hand and old houses so renovation might come into play, so it is really kind of looking at what society cares about and what your demographic cares about and you tailor your idea to that.

TV production companies invest a lot of time and money in idea creation, with development teams hired to come up with the next big commission by searching for the latest trends and social habits. They trawl all the news outlets and social media sites for inspiration and have regular brainstorming sessions. TV channels also guide TV producers by hosting industry sessions where they spell out their requirements, the gaps in their schedule and what types of programmes they are specifically looking to commission.

TV executives are always on the lookout for creative people to join their development teams. Having a broad interest in the world around you will help you to think beyond your immediate world, as Rebecca Yang explains:

> The ability to innovate is very important. I think people who are really good at what they do genuinely have a broad interest in the arts, in film, in movies. It helps because all these interests can help you to think creatively and inspire you and to put your plans into action, so I think a broad interest is very important for somebody to work in television.

So how do you become a creative ideas person? Is this a skill you can learn? Michael Michalko, in his book *Thinkertoys*, a handbook of creative-thinking techniques, thinks creativity starts with self belief:

A CEO of a major publishing company was concerned about the lack of creativity among his editorial and marketing staffs. He hired a group of high-priced psychologists to find out what differentiated the creative employees from the others. After studying the staff for one year, the psychologists discovered only one difference between the two groups. The creative people believed they were creative and the less creative people believed they were not … The psychologists recommended instituting a simple two-part program designed to change the belief system of those that thought they were not creative. The CEO agreed, and within a year, the uncreative people became many times more creative than the original creative group.[1]

So what can we learn from this? It's all about attitude – self-affirmation: anyone can be creative if they believe they are. It may sound cheesy but start right now by looking in the mirror and saying out loud 'I'm creative'. Write it down and also visualise yourself successfully creating groundbreaking ideas for television. Once you believe you are creative you need to start acting like a 'creative' person.

What we see, what we smell, what we taste and what we hear can all help to engender ideas, from conversations overheard in cafes, to artefacts at an exhibition. Ideas are everywhere and we can take inspiration from a vast array of sources from blogs to politics, the theatre, music or nature. To become a successful TV programme-generator, Karl Warner, Managing Director of Electric Ray, and former BBC Commissioning Editor says you have to work at it: 'get rested, take in all sorts of stimulus, challenge your assumptions and be prepared to sweat the idea.' It might help you to collate ideas in a visual scrapbook. To be creative you need to feel that you can come up with good and bad ideas and not worry about getting it wrong, so don't discount anything – from the ridiculous to the sublime. You need to be fearless, daring and courageous, and not feel scared of failing. Karl Warner has this advice for anyone wanting to work in a development team: 'You need a sense of fun and curiosity. Excellent analytical skills and writing skills. And a very thick skin!'

The Audience

By now you should start to have a broad range of ideas but how do you go about structuring them into something that you can present to a TV commissioner? To help you hone your idea you should think about your audience and never lose sight of who your audience is. You need to ask yourself: 'who does this idea appeal to?' Rarely will an idea appeal to everyone so you need to be specific and clearly establish a target audience. Understanding your audience is key to creating a great idea. You need to know your audience. What time would this show work? What channel or market would it suit? Each is clearly distinct. E4 is a youth-skewed channel and feels very different in look and content from ITV, which is much more of a mainstream family-friendly channel. Analyse TV schedules and look at the trade magazine *Broadcast*'s top shows by category. See if you can spot any trends or patterns or gaps in the market. For example, if you are making a kids' show you need to define what age range of kids – under six? Six to twelve? Is the programme for boys, girls, or both genders? Or do you want mums and dads to enjoy watching this too? Break the audience down and imagine a typical viewer for your show. You can even create a short profile of the perfect viewer. For a kids' studio drama about life in a dance school you might imagine the following:

<u>Sophie, age ten, from Chester</u>

Likes:	Horses, acting and chocolate
Dislikes:	Heights, spiders and school!
Watches:	YouTube tutorials, CBBC, Nickelodeon, *Got Talent*
Wants to be:	An actress or singer when she grows up

That way, throughout the idea formation stage you can ask your-self: 'will Sophie like this?' What is this offering her that is new and exciting and that she hasn't seen before? Building a profile can be a useful starting point.

Now Try This

Who do you imagine is the perfect viewer for the following shows? Write a short character profile for:

▸ *Channel 4 News*;
▸ *Coronation Street*;
▸ *Teletubbies*;
▸ *Big Brother*.

It's useful to share your ideas and see what other people think of them. Ask friends, family and work colleagues for their opinions. Posing questions on social media sites can be a useful tool to gather opinions and develop your ideas further. It's hard to know whether your idea is good until you've shared it.

With a script you can do a read-through and see how it flows. Reading a script on a piece of paper is very different to hearing someone read it out loud. Does it flow? If it's supposed to be funny – is it? If you're doing a game show you need to make sure your contestants understand the rules and that it's not overly complicated for the audience to understand. Ideas can sound straightforward on paper but in reality can be difficult to pull off. It's important to make sure you rehearse with real people. If it's a game show, make sure the rules can't be broken. Always play the game with the target age group to test out the format and check that it works, the rules are clear and importantly that the people taking part in your trial run enjoyed taking part and it excited them. Jeopardy is important whatever the genre as it keeps the audience tuned in. The audience should be engaged and want to see what happens next.

Some people worry that their ideas are going to get stolen by unscrupulous TV producers or commissioners and are too scared to tell anyone their ideas, but thinking like this will prevent your ideas from ever getting made. Dom Bird has this to say:

Ideas getting stolen – drives me crazy! It's one of the single most frustrating things. When people claim that it demonstrates a real naivety. I don't doubt in some point in history that has happened, but hand on heart, it's just not how we work. And I also believe that when someone has an idea and then we commissioned something that feels like their idea, they do genuinely believe their idea might have been stolen. I get how that works, but it isn't the case, we have ideas that are similar all the time and quite often when you analyse it (we have the luxury of being able to analyse it because we get all the ideas in we can see it), quite often there is a pattern because there has been something in the paper, something zeitgeisty, because a big event is coming up, so something quite subtle has happened which makes five people think of an idea, they will send it in to us, and if we commission one, four people are left potentially thinking that was their idea. We are very professional about it and I think they need to be professional about it. The other advice is, like anything in life, you have to share your idea and you have to ultimately trust that people will do the right thing otherwise you might as well not work in the business, you have to accept that there is a level of trust.

TV has been around for decades and we are all consuming the same media, so it is easy to think that everything has been done already and that it's impossible to come up with an original idea. To some extent this may be true, but there are ways around this. All genres need to innovate to offer audiences something new. For example, in sitcoms, breaking the fourth wall to speak to the audience as in *Miranda*, or adding celebrities to a format such as *Strictly Come Dancing*, or coming up with new ways to interact with your audience, such as adding live shows to a soap like *EastEnders*, or embedding additional content onto other platforms such as 90-second news items to explain a complicated story.

Something that is always unique is personal experience. We all have different life experiences. Creative writing teachers often advise their students to write from their own experience as this has the benefit of being a world they know intimately, as well as allowing them to personalise their stories and make them distinct. Can you use your life experience to make an idea seem original? Can you think of a new way to update an old idea? It's important to offer something that feels new and fresh rather than what has already come before – so you need to add a twist and make it innovative. You can improve your creativity by utilising different thinking techniques – these are not just used in the film and TV world but in all creative industries and in universities to improve innovation. What follows is not a definitive list but offers you a flavour of things that you might want to try out and explore further during your development phase:

Lateral thinking – this is a term created by psychologist Edward de Bono (1933)[2] and is a method used to develop creativity in a wide range of companies and educational institutions. It involves looking at problems from unusual perspectives in groups or individually, with the aim of stretching your imagination to 'think outside the box' before reaching a solution that is unexpected and effective.

Mind maps[3] – you may already be familiar with mind maps as they are commonly used in education to brainstorm ideas by visualising ideas and seeing how they connect. Mind maps are very easy to do. You start by writing a single word at the centre of a piece of paper and from there you work outwards, connecting and grouping words or pictures via curved lines and with a range of colours to help stimulate your mind and enhance your imagination.

Blue-sky thinking – this is a useful technique to use for group work. It involves bouncing ideas off each other. You need to feel that you are in a supportive group and all ideas should be welcomed. It can help to probe each other with questions such as those used by journalists sniffing out a story – who, why, what, where, when, how – and this will help you to hone your idea and come up with an action plan to move forward with.

You should also think about where you have got your best ideas. Is it when you go for a walk or when you're having a cup of tea in a busy café? It is useful to reflect on what works for you – quiet or noisy locations, inside or outside – and change your location to spark your imagination. Many people say that their favourite place to think of ideas is the bathroom – not surprisingly this is one of the few places in your home that you won't be interrupted! Writers and artists typically escape to a retreat in the countryside that allows them to get their creative juices flowing and are inspired by a stunning landscape. Development teams in production companies do similar so-called 'away days' to encourage creative thinking.

Karl Warner shares his brainstorming technique exercises:

1. Stare out of the window – get into a zone – on a bike, swimming, in the shower, staring at a fire – like a form of meditation which allows your brain to expand and think of anything that comes to mind.

2. Opposites attract – take elements of a quiz show – what are the usual elements? Now do the opposite. On one side of paper write what usually happens and on the other side write what the opposite is. For example, friendly host versus a mean host. *The Weakest Link* felt new and exciting at the time, as we weren't used to seeing someone like Anne Robinson being rude to the contestants. *Who Wants to be a Millionaire?* was a great success and Channel 4 turned this on its head with *Million Pound Drop* by starting with a million pounds and trying to keep hold of it.

3. Unusual triggers – go through old *Radio Times* or TV, newspaper listings. *Fear Factor* versus *Strictly come Dancing* or *Rambo* versus *Lambing Live* – what would that look like? If an idea makes you laugh, don't dismiss it.
4. Chaos – pick names or words out of a hat and link them together.

Formats dominate the TV schedules. They are repeatable, cross-territories and have the potential to be highly profitable. Examples of formats include the game show *Deal or No Deal*, factual cooking contest *The Great British Bake Off*, talent show *The X Factor* and sitcom *The Office*. It is much harder to make money in TV with a one-off idea – commissioners are looking for returnable, longer-running series and the holy grail of ideas is a big international hit show as David Williams, BBC Creative Director of Entertainment North, explains:

> The big global entertainment hits that work are more valued now than ever. The end goal for any studio entertainment piece nowadays is for it to be licensed as a format or able to work as a finished product and play in different territories and often now they are built around the model that sometimes needs a number of different territories to make them financially work. Shows such as *Total Wipeout* where they have a big production base now have other territories come in and use that same facility. *I'm a Celebrity* jungle does that, and companies come in and use the same facilities. So you are able to get a large-scale show together through its ability to reach other audiences out of the home one and these formats, entertainment, it travels, probably better than anything else, better than drama. [There are] fewer national traits in entertainment, it is much more universal, so I think absolutely that is always the end goal.

Once you have a hit, commissioners will be looking for it to roll out into other territories and so you need to create a bible that explains all the ins and outs of your show. Who is involved in the production – including an idea of how many people would need to work on the programme, the schedule, the budget and the studio set details. This provides a blueprint that is sold with the programme but each programme does need to take in the nuances of a particular territory and adjust the idea for that market as Rebecca Yang explains when talking about the *Top Model* franchise in China:

> First of all in the American or any Western versions it has a very individual heroism, it's Tara Banks' show or in the UK it is Elle MacPherson's show but in China it is not about the host, it is about the models, it is

their show. So we have changed that, and secondly all the challenges in the show, all the photo shoots, these are completely tailored to the appreciation of the Chinese audience and also the storytelling; we have five Chinese scriptwriters writing the whole thing – it is more scripted reality really. We are trying to tap into what the Chinese people want from an inspiring journey so there was a lot of adaptation needed.

Formatted television is ideas-driven and a good format can be a hit all over the world. But having the idea is the easy part: developing it to the stage where it's ready for production takes a lot of organisation and hard work. But is there a foolproof method of creating an exciting, saleable television series? Dom Bird at Channel 4 says:

Good ideas are usually simple. The important thing to remember is that a simple idea doesn't mean simple to execute. Simple ideas are usually the hardest to execute, so a clear premise helps a quick commission but quite often that then means the production is massively complicated. So broadly there is a pattern that good ideas are simple in premise, rather than execution.

Each format can be broken down into format points. So for example in a studio film show you might have the following items in every episode:

▸ The title sequence;
▸ The intro, PTC (presenter piece-to-camera);
▸ The body, interviews and VTs (film clips);
▸ The outro (conclusion).

You would then break this down further to consider which elements can be identical, such as the set design, lighting, direction and music, and the elements that would be tailored for the local market, such as the presenters, crew and production team. These elements form a blueprint of what the show is.

You need to make sure that your programme can sustain the slot time length – whether that's 30 minutes or an hour. Kids programmes generally tend to be shorter so there are typically 10- to 15-minute slots available here. Look at the schedules once you have an idea. Where do you think it would best sit? Does it complement an existing show? Some ideas sound promising but in reality they are not meaty enough to last longer than a 1- to 5-minute-long segment, which might work really well as a VT, in a magazine format such as *The One Show* or as a stand-alone sketch on a comedy show, but not as an entire programme. The other really important thing to remember is to include a beginning, middle and end. Every genre needs jeopardy to engage the audience. So what are commissioners looking for? The following is a brief guideline provided by commissioners at conferences we have attended over the years:

‣ **Audience reaction** – commissioners say that they want to know how a TV programme will make them feel, whether it's sadness, anger, happiness or laughter. It is much better to provoke an emotional response than none at all.
‣ **Identify the channel** – know how your idea fits into the channel and make a case for why it is a good fit for the channel.
‣ **Casting** – you might not be able to afford or secure your wish list but making some suggestions can provide a guide as to what you would like.
‣ **Idea execution** – who are the key crew, what technical equipment do you need, which locations?
‣ **Visuals** – TV is a visual medium – bring the idea to life by explaining how it will be made (the style/tone/mood).
‣ **Why now?** – why is this idea ripe for TV now? What is the avenue into the idea or the zeitgeist topic that will get people hooked?

Multiplatform

Don't just look at the main broadcasters – there are lots of opportunities in the multiplatform world for making content for different platforms, tablets, mobiles, and mini web-series. You could also think about your own channel, vlogging, or making shorts that would work well with existing programmes, or offering additional content or games, as drama director Jet Wilkinson states:

> I think new media and interactive media have created a whole new set of jobs for people and new windows of opportunity to be able to make additional material. It's a very interesting and evolving part of the industry and it's certainly expanded the industry.

The positives of airing your own programmes online are that you can do things your way, there are no restrictions on the length, no interference from commissioners or executive producers, and you can shoot on any device, including your phone. The disadvantages are who will watch it? It's much more likely that it will have a smaller reach than broadcast TV; however, there is the possibility of it going viral and getting shared around the globe! You would be working on your own and wouldn't receive the support or mentorship of being part of the industry. It is also becoming harder to get noticed and make your mark with so many people now having their own channels or posting videos. The quality is unlikely to be as good as a broadcast show with a big team and budget. Despite all this it's still an option and the more films you make, the better you will become!

Once you've come up with lots of ideas you need to think about which ones you feel most passionate about. If the idea does not excite you, it is highly unlikely to excite a commissioner. You need to check that it is actually achievable. Do your research – has there been anything like this before? If there has, don't be put off – how can you put a new spin on it and dress it up so that it appears fresh? You need to start thinking about the logistics of your idea. How will it work? Is it realistic to make with your budget? How feasible is it? What are the health and safety implications? And importantly will it resonate with your audience?

Make a shortlist of ideas that you are most excited about and think have the most potential. Now it is time to go to the next step – writing a proposal.

Proposal Writing

Once you have thoroughly researched your idea and know the target audience and channel you can start to write a proposal, the industry document used to sell your TV idea to a commissioning editor. It should be conversational and colourful rather than overly wordy or academic in tone. Typically it is one to three pages long with relevant images and headlines. It's not a treatment, which is a much longer document that goes into extensive detail of all aspects of your programme once a commissioner has shown interest.

It's a helpful way for you to clarify your thoughts about your show, what it's really about and how you'll make it.

There are no hard and fast rules for how to structure a proposal but the following is a general outline of points commissioners look for:

Title page – the title page is your chance to make a statement and grab the commissioner's attention. It should contain visual branding to make your idea stand out. Essential things to include on the title page are the title, tag line, appropriate image(s) and your contact details (name, address, email and phone number). It always surprises us how many people forget to do this!

Make it clear what the genre is, for example a quiz show, a comedy panel show, and who it is for (target audience). Include the channel that you think it would most suit and the slot, such as BBC One, weekdays 17:00.

When you send it out to commissioners you will then have to make sure that you change these details accordingly. An ITV exec will not give you the time of day if they see that it went to the BBC first and they rejected it!

Also remember to include page numbers.

Title – make it stand out. It should sum up the programme and be catchy. The trend is for shorter titles that fit on the EPG (electronic programme guide that you see on the screen) like *The Cube, Ninja Warriors,* or *Top Gear*. It is important to know what commissioners are looking for. Read *Broadcast*, the industry trade magazine for everything happening in the TV world.

Tagline/logline – a single sentence you use to describe your programme. If you can't describe it in one sentence you will find it hard to pitch. Most famously legend has it that *Alien* was commissioned on three words – *Jaws* in space.

Who is it for? – time slot, target audience, duration/number of episodes, for example 19:00–20:00, ITV1 Saturday night family entertainment, 7 × 60 minutes

Summary – a short and snappy paragraph of the idea – imagine a newspaper billing. Enough information to get the audience to watch and the commissioner to greenlight it.

The body of the proposal should expand on characters, what the programme is about, what we'll see.

Synopsis – give a programme outline, including its Unique Selling Point (USP). Who's involved? – the characters, talent, story, themes. What will we see/why should we care? Show there is a story – ask yourself is it clear what the story is about? What are the key scenes and does it have a beginning, middle and end? What is at stake? Remember, every programme needs jeopardy to hold the viewer's attention.

Key players – provide an idea of who your principal cast/presenters/contributors will be and who the key crew are to help sell your idea. Some channels have a preference for using certain names.

Locations – where is your production going to be set? What impact does this have on your schedule?

Style – what will it look and feel like? For example, presenter-led, studio, multi-cam, single-cam, and archive. Explain your approach, the format and tone.

Interactivity – think of the interactive potential of your idea and how you can engage your audience on other platforms.

Why now? – a question that commissioners love to ask. Explain why it is relevant and why it should be commissioned now.

Images – choose images that complement your title and visually sum up the style of your idea. Be aware of copyright – take the photo yourself or check online sites for images that can be downloaded for free.

Proposal Writing Tips

▸ Use visually striking images to bring your idea to life.
▸ Don't make it word-heavy. This is not an academic essay! Use headings to break it down and guide the reader.
▸ Have a killer title to grab the commissioner's attention.
▸ Do a spellcheck and read-through for typos and grammatical errors.
▸ Make it very clear who the audience is.
▸ Give a clear idea of what you will see and how it will be shot.
▸ Remember to suggest casting ideas.
▸ Restrict it to one to three pages. Make it clear and concise. Avoid waffle!

▸ Use the present or future tense – avoid 'might', 'maybe'.
▸ Remember to have a USP – what differentiates this from anything similar?

Summary

Finally, don't give up – you will need to come up with a lot of ideas before you hit on something that actually works and you get the call to meet a commissioner. Practise your idea on friends and family, gauge their reactions and get ready to pitch!

Now Try This

Now attempt to answer the following questions for your own original studio show:

1. Who is in your idea? – the characters/cast. Write bullet-point biographies.
2. What is your idea? What happens? Think about the hook and the outcome.
3. Where will you shoot? – choice of location(s).
4. When can filming begin? – are there any restrictions/is it event-linked? Dates and times.
5. Why now? Think USP.
6. How will it make the audience feel emotionally?

3

GETTING COMMISSIONED

So now you have an idea, but how are you going to get it on television? In the UK the traditional way is to get a broadcaster (such as ITV, BBC, Channel 4, Sky etc.) to fund your production before you begin filming. Broadcasters have an original programming budget, which they divide between genre commissioning editors. Each commissioner is responsible for a different time of day within the viewing schedule and works to specific tariffs, with daytime programmes typically receiving smaller budgets than prime-time evening viewing shows.

Dom Bird, Head of Formats, Music and Education at Channel 4 and former executive producer of Dragons Den and producer on *Strictly Come Dancing*, explains how the system works:

> The model is remarkably similar in all the main UK broadcasters, which is there is a channel controller for all the individual channels and underneath that, genre commissioning editors. Ultimately the controller has responsibility for the channel, with a number of different departments such as a factual department, entertainment department, a features department, formats, drama and comedy all reporting to them.

Budgets vary between departments. There is no point pitching a multimillion-pound-per-episode idea to a daytime commissioner who has a much smaller budget to use. Daytime programming is traditionally a good fit with studio productions. Look at the EPG and work out how many studio shows you can spot that run during the day. Studios can cost-effectively produce high-volume runs; think ITV's *This Morning* and *Jeremy Kyle* – they will commission 200-plus episodes in a run and these contracts are worth millions of pounds.

David Williams, BBC Creative Director of Entertainment North, explains the role of a commissioning editor:

> Commissioning Editors are the gate-keepers to any Broadcaster. Whilst the degree of editorial freedom that they enjoy differs from place to place they are all ultimately tasked with answering the brief set by Channel Controllers and populating it with the best possible content. Initially they take the brief or vision set by Channel Controllers and either seek out ideas proactively or filter those that come to them. They act as the conduit between the Controller and the production company. Once an idea has been commissioned, their aim is to ensure that the final programme is editorially, financially and legally sound and suitable for broadcast. They are there as well to support the production company through the inevitable challenges that arise and, as they're removed from the day to day minutiae of making the programme, are able to offer a broader perspective on the editorial that can often be hard to maintain by those working more closely on the project.

As well as the broadcaster route there are all kinds of digital possibilities to host your programme, such as Netflix and Amazon Prime, as well as films produced just for the web on YouTube and VICE for example. Online, the length of the show is not always so restrictive as you do not have to keep to a strict schedule. Presenters Jeremy Clarkson and co from the BBC's global hit *Top Gear* are a good example of the power of these newer digital routes for content creation, as the presenters have switched sides to create a rival car magazine show for Amazon Prime, with a big production budget. There is also nothing to stop you creating your own online channel to screen your content – although you will be funding this yourself, it may help you and your idea get noticed.

Typically to even get a meeting with broadcasters in the USA, as the producer you have to have an agent. The structure is slightly different with some different titles for roles, such as the 'showrunner', that we would refer to in the UK as the series producer, who drives the ideas for the show.

Most broadcasters have a commissioning portal, which provides information on briefs, tariffs and how to submit ideas. Some are happy for you to contact them directly. Dom Bird explains how the pitching process works:

Each department has a team of commissioning editors. People can pitch to us in any number of ways, we hold face-to-face meetings every day and people will email us ideas, so people can get hold of us in any number of ways. There is no rule that you have to be a registered company to submit an idea, we can receive unsolicited ideas from individuals. I would say it is helpful if you are aligned to a company with some sort of reputation or some sort of ability to deliver because whilst the idea is the most important thing, ability to deliver it is also critical. There are instances in the past where people who don't have the infrastructure, we have helped join them up with production companies, but I would say people can put themselves on a slightly faster track if they align themselves to an infrastructure to help them deliver a good idea.

If you do not feel ready to set up your own Indie (independent production company) you can approach existing production companies to see if they would like to work with you on your idea. Do not get blinded by pound signs here. Typical deals in this area will net you around 30 per cent of the production fee (3 per cent of the overall budget – if you are lucky – and sometimes less) so this may not be a get-rich-quick scheme, but it's a good way of developing your production portfolio with limited risk to the individual. Either way, if you have an amazing idea the broadcaster will partner you with a company if needs be and find a way to help you get it made.

Another way to get noticed is to attend film and television festivals. Often they run pitching competitions to win development money, which is a great way to get on the decision makers' radars. Key television festivals in the UK like Sheffield Doc/Fest and Edinburgh International TV Festival (EITF) are great places to learn about the industry and rub shoulders with the channel executives. The EITF runs a prestigious talent scheme for new entrants called The Network, and getting on to this scheme can really help fast-track your career.

Campbell Glennie, Director of Talent Schemes at Edinburgh International TV Festival, says:

Festivals are the one time the great and good are out in the wild with no gatekeepers in the way. This environment favours the talented and the bold – senior execs are always looking for new voices and new talent and will give their time and, more importantly, attention, more readily. A talented student with the right amount of preparation can turn a festival into a real springboard. I know students who've gone home with jobs, development deals, even commissions from festivals. Taking part in a live pitch competition can be an excellent way to get recognition for you and your idea. Never underestimate the power of getting your name and face out there at festivals. A confident pitch in a room full of your potential bosses is an invaluable opportunity, regardless of whether you win or not.

There are other routes to fund your television production such as the use of interactivity, brand funding and crowdfunding. Interactivity is using things like the vote lines, where the viewer decides who is eliminated or wins, and this typically sees a percentage of the money generated being shared between the broadcaster and production company. Competition lines work in a similar way.

Brand funding is relatively new to UK television, but widely used overseas and in films. This is where brands and products pay to feature in a programme or film. The film franchise *James Bond* is the master of this, using the brands featured as part of the storyline rather than feeling like an obvious advertorial. *Big Brother* UK is another example, using some brand funding in their series. Watch an episode and see if you can spot them.

Crowdfunding, as the name suggests, involves getting lots of different people or organisations to invest in you and your idea. Social media has really aided the development of this, as you can reach masses of people and get them excited about your idea. There are many dedicated websites and companies like Indiegogo and Kickstarter that act as funding platforms for creative projects.

Okay, so you have worked out which platform best suits your idea, your funding route, and have either formed or partnered with a production company – but how are you going to get the commissioning editor to notice your idea?

David Williams provides some perspective:

> In BBC Entertainment alone we receive over 200 ideas a week. Sifting through this is time consuming. You never want to be the one to say no to a big hit that a rival channel snaps up. So painstakingly we read every one. We can tell quite quickly by the title and a couple of lines in if this is something we are interested in. It may be a good idea, but we may already have three shows in development that are similar or it may not fit with the channel's agenda.

Remember many broadcast channels are working around 18 months in advance. They already have on-the-shelf programmes ready to air or have agreed multi-year deals with big prime-time hits that will tie-up that slot for some time. Think about ITV for example. Already we know the news is scheduled to happen every day at 6pm and 10pm so those slots are gone. Then the long-running soaps have most of the 7.30pm/8pm/8.30pm slots. Once you start identifying these fixed points you can see there is limited availability to screen new series.

Also consider that what we are talking about now may not be relevant in 18 months/two years by the time your show finally airs. General elections, big sporting events like the Olympics and fashion trends can sway what works for a channel. A good example is the popular property-buying series that were a staple of the television schedule in the early 2000s – until the economic crash happened which then rendered them irrelevant to viewers. This included shows like Channel 4's *Property Ladder*, which was renamed *Property Snakes and Ladders* to try and reflect the mood of the time better. So try and think ahead. If our screens are filled with game shows now, will quiz shows be ready for a return the following year?

Commissioners are always looking ahead to the next big thing. They initially prefer a short description of your idea, with a strong title and maybe some idea of the talent you envisage presenting or starring in your show. They want to quickly get a handle on your idea and be able to make a decision as to where this may fit on their channel. If they already have ten studio shows on weddings, yours as the eleventh will not work no matter how good it is. Condensing your idea can be quite a challenge, as you want to include everything, every twist and turn of your brilliant idea, but less really is more. Even the most complicated of ideas should be able to be told in two lines.

Famous entertainment presenters Ant and Dec said at the EITF in 2012 that, for them, the mark of a good idea is being able to say *this is the show where…* you win the ads, can win a million all by choosing red or black etc. If you cannot sum it up in this way then it probably is not a great idea.

A strong title can make your idea memorable and stand out – it's an area that broadcasters and producers agonise over, often changing time and time again. With competition from hundreds of channels, there is an appetite for titles to do what they say on the tin. Viewers want to know what they are getting so they can make a quick decision as to whether to watch or not. Remember, the number of characters which fit across the EPG banner is about 32, so shorter titles work better.

Dom Bird explains more on the importance of having a strong title:

> The killer title is overrated I think at the point of development. The title is critical when the programme goes over the EPG. We change titles all the time quite close to transmission because that is the point when we will focus on what will bring an audience in. For me, obviously killer titles are fun, and encouraging, but I wouldn't commission a programme just because it had a great title. I look at the programmes that we have commissioned over the last year, successful commissions, most of them were pitched as a sentence or a paragraph initially and most of them can be boiled down to one line. The ten page treatment is completely unnecessary, sometimes it is necessary later in a stage, but not necessary in the beginning. I know you need to refine it or it might not be a very good idea if you can't explain it in one line.

If you have the buy-in from key talent that the funder likes, it can help fast-track your idea. Posy Brewer is a voice-over artist and actor and has worked with clients including BBC, Coca-Cola, Sky, Cadbury, Nickelodeon, Disney, Channel 5 and ITV:

> Getting a voice and/or acting talent on board at an early stage is always good. It can help shape the project and bring a real personality to the piece. Having experienced talent can help advise and give you ideas on how the project sounds and feels from the 'on-screen' perspective. It is a collaborative effort. Personally when I have been lined up to do projects from the start it helps to build the relationship with the team and ensures you have a real understanding of what is needed. A voice can change the whole project – it enhances the mood and style, giving it a three-dimensional aspect.

Dom Bird says:

> Talent is very important. At Channel 4 we support new talent. Where people need to be savvy is that we (working at the channel) look at Channel 4 and E4 and consider them to be distinct from all the other channels – so it shows a lack of knowledge to come in with completely inappropriate talent just because they are famous or to confuse E4 with BBC3 or MTV. So I think talent has to be appropriate to the channel but most importantly the idea has to be appropriate

to the channel and you have to understand the nuance between all the different channels; Channel 4 and ITV and E4 and BBC3, and that is the biggest stumbling block I think for the people submitting new ideas.

The Pitch

If you have managed to get a commissioning editor interested in your idea, the next stage will be a pitch. Let's deconstruct what a pitch is. A pitch is a primary sales tool for your idea. It gives a snapshot of your idea and can build excitement around the project. It is also a primary sales tool for you. In any ideas pitch you are also selling yourself. Do they believe in you? Trust you to make the idea a reality? Ideas and contacts are the currency of the industry.

When thinking about your idea and getting 'pitch-ready', practise articulating it in 25 words or less. Have a go now. Explain what your favourite television programme is about in just a couple of lines. This condensed style needs to plant your idea visually and create interest. This type of pitch is often referred to as an 'elevator pitch'. Imagine you step into the lift by chance with the top television commissioner, you have the length of a lift ride to sell your idea before they can either escape to the safety of their office or sign you up for a meeting to discuss more!

As already mentioned, a good pitch will usually have a catchy title, a memorable log or tag line (*the show where you win the ads* etc.), some idea of the talent involved and a clear understanding of the audience.

David Williams explains what makes a good pitch:

> Whether it's a documentary, a sitcom or an entertainment show, a pitch needs to provide compelling answers to the basic key questions: what is the idea, what will you see, why does this idea work for this channel and why should we make this now? The best pitches answer all of these questions clearly, comprehensively and imaginatively alongside delivering a great idea that gets a commissioner excited!

Lyn Burgess is the founder of Magic Key Partnership, a business coach for film, television and digital media industries, and works with people to get pitch-ready. She says:

Most common mistakes people make when they are pitching is not enough preparation. It is absolutely key. This includes being completely relaxed with your treatment, synopsis and elevator pitch so that they come across in the right way. Additionally, researching the person you are going to meet is also important. Make sure you are in rapport with the person you are meeting, a lot of people hate 'small talk', but it is necessary. If the decision maker hasn't connected with you, they might not connect with your project. Don't get defensive. Yes, we all know you think it's the best thing since sliced bread, and it's your baby, but at some stage you have to let go. If someone suggests changing something, always agree to 'have a think about that'. Always check with the decision maker as to what the next step is, at the end of the meeting so that you don't walk out the room wondering what's next.

If you are able to secure a pitch meeting, make sure you make the most of your time. Think about your branding. A picture or a logo can say more than a thousand words. Start building a brand identity for your programme idea to make it more memorable and believable. If you have been developing your idea then include any relevant support media – for example filmed clips, audio, stills and slides – to help bring your idea to life. Remember if the commissioning editor likes your idea, they will then need to sell it on to their bosses to get their buy-in – so they need to have as much detail as possible to help create excitement. Maybe leave a flyer or something memorable related to your idea to keep it fresh in the commissioning editor's mind.

So are you ready to pitch?

▸ Do you know your pitch inside out? Practise on friends – get them to recite back to you what you said. Do they understand the idea?
▸ Have you researched whom you are pitching to? There are many stories of people in interviews and pitches being negative about a programme the person they are pitching to has worked on!
▸ Be positive and show your passion and enthusiasm.
▸ How have you set up your pitch? Laptop? Website? Be prepared for all eventualities. If technology fails, have paper copies and a back-up plan.
▸ Engage your audience by telling a compelling story to make your idea come alive.
▸ Practice makes perfect!

The Taster Tape

To accompany your idea and pitch you may be asked for a 'taster tape' or 'sizzle reel'. This is a short film (usually under ten minutes in length) that gives a flavour of your idea, which may highlight the lead character, location or format points. This helps bring your idea to life and inspire confidence. Although it does not have to be broadcast quality, be warned that if it does not look professional it can undermine your idea.

David Williams says:

> Technology has increasingly allowed producers to make tasters for low costs, making it the norm to do so. I think as a growing trend, it has its benefits for both parties. Where an idea depends on talent or contributors or perhaps a technical or visual device, then a good taster is always going to sell that idea better to a commissioner than a piece of paper. The very process of cutting the taster can also be useful in itself, in helping hone the idea. It forces producers to interrogate an idea more thoroughly than they perhaps would do just writing a paper treatment.

If you are making a taster tape/sizzle reel make sure you have a powerful opening. You do not necessarily need to start at the beginning of the story; set-ups can take time, so go straight to the argument, the marriage proposal or whatever it is that makes your idea seem a must-see. Shock, humour and emotional cliffhangers can all help to engage your audience – you only have a few minutes to make your impact, so make every second count. Start strong and end stronger! End on a cliffhanger and tease the commissioners – *give me the money to make it and you'll get your ending!* Make sure you add some production values where appropriate. Music or a logo can all help make your taster tape look dynamic and sell your concept.

Dom Bird says:

> Taster tapes are very important a lot of the time, but at Channel 4 we will quite often fund the taster tape if we are at that stage of the idea. Taster tapes are required much more than they used to be. It obviously helps visualise the idea but it can be expensive. Nobody wants to deliver a substandard taster tape because that can kill an idea but it is very expensive to deliver a good one.

Making a taster of your idea is also one of the best ways to retain copyright in your idea – a proof of concept. People are often scared to share or talk about their ideas – don't be. If you don't talk about them they will never get made!

If You Are Not Successful

Don't worry – try again. Even the leading production companies have to generate hundreds of ideas to achieve their wins. If you are rejected, don't take it personally. Pick yourself up and think about how you can reshape your idea for another channel. Maybe by changing the title or the talent it could work and even become better than the original. Sometimes it's just about timing. There are many stories of big hits that took years to get commissioned. Global hit *Who Wants to be a Millionaire?* took many years to be commissioned, but it was worth the wait as it ended up being sold in over 100 countries.

If you are successful, what happens next? If you are being funded by a broadcaster you will be asked to submit a detailed budget to their Business Affairs department explaining how you will make the programme. Similarly if you are using investors or a different business model, such as interactivity or crowdfunding, you will still need to put in place detailed planning to demonstrate how you are going to physically make the idea.

Summary

‣ Decide your funding route. How are you paying for your programme?
‣ Decide the channel that suits your idea best and match the talent and style accordingly.
‣ Research whom you are pitching to – understand what they are looking for.
‣ Make sure you have a strong title and an elevator pitch ready for your idea.
‣ If there is a sign of interest, consider making a taster tape.

Now Try This

1. Create an elevator pitch for an original studio show, thinking about the channel or platform it would play on. Sum up your idea in 60 seconds, then in 30 seconds, then in 10 seconds. Time each other. Does your idea still make sense? Is it exciting?

2. Now tweak your original idea for a different channel. What would you need to do to make it fit Channel 4 if your original idea suited ITV? This is all about understanding your audience and the channel's brand values.

So you have been successful and won your first commission. Now the work begins. Read on to learn how to begin production planning and how to translate your idea into the studio.

4

THE STUDIO ENVIRONMENT

You have your idea and are ready to go but how will you actually make your programme? In this chapter you will find out everything you need to know about the studio environment. Studios can seem daunting. Everyone has a specific role to play to ensure it runs like a well-oiled machine. By the end of this chapter you will have a much clearer idea of how the studio operates, who does what and why.

The studio is where a programme comes together and the action happens. The studio comprises what is referred to as the 'studio floor' and the 'gallery' or 'control room'. The studio is an empty vessel to begin with, providing a flexible space for sets to be created, from simple backdrops to the most outlandish. Think how different the set of Channel 5's daytime talk show *The Wright Stuff* is compared to the sparkly razzamatazz of the BBC's *Strictly Come Dancing* or the cosy coffee shop set in Warner Bros. Television's *Friends* Central Perk. The studio provides the face of a show and helps to give it a personality, as Job Rabkin, Commissioning Editor, *Channel 4 News Investigations* explains:

> The studio is absolutely essential and is the heart of the show. The studio is really the front of *Channel 4 News* and what you see. So what the studio looks like and what the studio feels like is absolutely essential to our identity, who we are, what we are about.

Studio Set

A lot of thought goes into how the studio set looks and the design has to fit the tone of the show and be in keeping with the channel's branding. Some long-running factual and entertainment shows undergo set décor relaunches every few years to keep up to date with trends, audience taste and to avoid looking dated. Some of these relaunches work better than others. A rebranding of BBC's *Today at Wimbledon* in 2015 was heavily criticised by the audience and critics when it moved from being a straightforward commentary show with a backdrop of the tennis courts, to a glamorous looking bar set-up with audience members in vision. The complaints were so great that the BBC reverted back to the original set structure – such is the power of the audience.

The studio floor is where the set is created by a team of riggers and art and production designers. It is also where all the cameras are. The number of cameras varies hugely. Studios can be used for single-camera shows and dramas, but also for multi-camera set-ups with anything from three cameras upwards. Technology is always advancing and on some programmes, such as *BBC News*, they no longer have cameras that are operated by people, but instead are robotically controlled with computer software.

The studio environment offers lots of opportunities with green screen or blue screen allowing producers and directors to bring any number of backdrops from anywhere in the world into the studio by using 'chroma-key', a production switcher, that allows the director to

Image 1 Studio gallery (Courtesy of *Channel 4 News*)

Image 2 *Coronation Street* sets

replace a background colour (typically blue or green) with anything they like; pre-recorded material, stills or a live video link. 3D worlds can also be created to help illustrate news, science or political stories, for example demonstrating election results, bringing something that might not at first sound very visual to life, on a grand scale.

Studio technology is constantly evolving. Shows previously shot in standard definition are now all required to be in high definition (a better-quality screen resolution) and the environment is tapeless, using hard drives and memory cards instead of video tapes. The popular children's series *Teletubbies* was originally broadcast on the BBC between 1997–2001 in standard definition and was revamped in late 2015. In the original series the exterior shots were filmed outside, but for the new series they required greater control of the schedule and so built a replica miniature set of Teletubbyland. They worked with a visual effects team to create computer-generated imagery (CGI) that, as executive producer Maddy Darrall puts it, 'made it look perfectly feasible to have an eight-foot Teletubby standing on the four-cm hill'. Director of Photography, Simon Reay, who worked on the original *Teletubbies* and the latest version, explains the benefits of shooting in the studio environment:

> The biggest change is having control of everything, especially the weather and that is part of the reason for shooting on a model – you could create a perfect set based on the original one but improve the use of space and make it easier for the Teletubby performers to move.

I remember Teletubbies could never get within six feet of the walls on the original set because they would hit their aerials on the roof!

The studio set is, on most programmes, a temporary structure and however good it looks, when the show ends it needs to be struck (taken down) so that the next programme can come in with their set. Many sets are made up of a series of 'flats', a frame panel that resembles a chain of wooden doors. These flats can then be dressed with wallpaper or painted to create any desired backdrop, and then carefully sourced props and furniture can be added creating an instant, believable world – whether it's Beale's café in *EastEnders* or a street scene in Warner Bros. Television's *2 Broke Girls*. The sets need to be adaptable, as they typically have to double up as more than one location. On Channel 5's talk show *The Wright Stuff*, the set is transformed completely every weekend into a working kitchen to make way for Channel 4's *Sunday Brunch*. If you can it is always a good idea to be an audience member on a studio show, so that you can see the mechanics of the studio environment close up for yourself and the vast lighting grid that hangs from the ceiling, the incredible detail of the set design and where the cameras are strategically placed to capture the action. There are a number of companies, such as Applause Store, that offer members of the public free tickets to shows recorded in front of an audience.

Job Roles – Who Does What?

It's very important that you have a sound understanding of all the job roles and studio etiquette so that you don't mistake the young-looking executive producer for the junior researcher! Once you know what everyone does and what their job responsibilities are, you will have a clearer idea of which roles you would be interested in doing and can map out how to get there.

Within the TV industry there is a wide range of job roles. By understanding how the different roles connect, you can begin to think about what your career path looks like. Here, we will give you an overview of the most common job roles on a studio TV show in the UK (as we've said, the USA has a slightly different structure and different names for jobs). This is not a definitive guide. There are some differences across genres and not all studio shows use multi-camera studio set-ups. Some low-budget studio productions can involve

Image 3 Studio floor

crew multitasking and taking on three or four roles, for example directing, vision mixing and rolling the VT, or hair and make-up, costume and floor managing.

Studio Crew

The crew roles typically refer to the technical and craft roles, all an essential part of the programme-making process. Typically, these roles are held by freelance staff that are hired for short periods of time. For example, a camera operator would typically be hired just for the shooting period, whereas a set designer would be brought onboard early on in the pre-production phase to create the set.

Production Team

The production team are the people who are typically employed on longer contracts to oversee the programme-making process, editorially, creatively and logistically, from beginning to end. The production team do the pre-production in their own office and relocate to the studio, setting up a temporary office for the duration of the shoot and rehearsal. The TV industry has a very hierarchical structure. In most cases people start at the bottom, as a runner, and have to work their way up by proving themselves to those above them in the pecking order. Sometimes students who have made productions at university or college think that they will be able to enter the TV industry at a higher level but this is rarely, if ever, the case. But don't be disheartened by the fact that you will most likely have to start at a junior level. This is a great training ground and if you work hard and impress you can have a meteoric job climb, seeming to go from runner to producer or director in no time. Anything is possible in telly. Werner Walian, producer of studio dramas *The Fresh Prince of Bel-Air* and *The Middle*, explains how people can move up the ranks:

> You need good people skills and to learn about all the other people who work on a show. Some of the people who work on a show could hire you on their show, and before you know it, the PA who was on this show is now their assistant and three years from now they might be producing or they might be writing. So the number one thing is to get in at that entry-level. The ones that do a good job, survive and move up. It's all do-able!

Graham Sherrington, director of *Top Gear*, *Grand Designs* and *The F-Word*, graduated from a university media production course and swiftly moved from being a runner on the soap *Emmerdale* to director at the age of 23! He offers these words of wisdom to anyone wanting to succeed in TV:

> From *Emmerdale* I left drama and moved into factual TV, starting as an assistant researcher on a satellite channel. From there I got a regional TV programme commissioned when I was quite young, 22, and then I became a director of that programme at 23 and I have been directing ever since! It's very easy to say that you want to be a director, or you want to be a production manager, but my biggest advice would be find out what those roles are and what they do and whether they fit with who you are and what you would like to do.

Executive Producer (EP)

The EP is the most senior position in the production team. They will have worked their way up through the ranks and have many years of programme-making experience and leadership, running the show. They hire key members of the team, have the final say on the editorial content of the show and have ultimate responsibility for delivering the show to the commissioning editor. Maddy Darrall, co-founder of independent production company Darrall Macqueen and EP of *Teletubbies*, offers her advice on what makes a good EP:

> I think you have got to have been a programme maker, and have a really good idea of everybody's role and be a good delegator and employ good people so that you can let them get along with their role without interfering. When you go into an edit, try not to make a show you might have conceived, but to see it through somebody else's eyes and make one or two comments that might help but let them have their own creative freedom to make a show for themselves.

Programme Editor

In news or talk show formats you will have a news editor or series editor of the show. They don't physically edit particular programmes, but editorially oversee the day-to-day running of the programmes. Working with them is an assistant editor who is their number two, and then the producer(s) and reporters for news shows, who are out in the field bringing in stories.

Producer

The producer is at the coalface of the programme decision-making and refers up to the executive producer when necessary. They are involved in all aspects of the show from the pre-production stage to post-production and delivery of the show – overseeing the editorial content and scripts, costumes, casting, filming and the edit. Werner Walian explains the challenges a producer faces:

> Basically, when a show starts up, the role of a producer starts from scratch. Everything has to be figured out – from designer, to set, to where to shoot the show, putting the crew together, working with the studio budget, working with the creative people and figuring out how we are going to produce the show.

Director

The director is in charge of the visuals and choreographing what is seen on the screen. They work closely with all parts of the production team and crew to convey their creative vision for the programme, from the set and costume designers to sound supervisors, lighting and scriptwriters. They may even write the scripts on some factual and entertainment shows. The director will need to work out how to shoot the script and will do this by breaking the script down and preparing a shot list. They are often involved in the casting process and are responsible for getting the best performances possible out of the talent (and putting any contributors at ease so that they don't clam up when the cameras start rolling).

Much of a director's job is done before the shoot and it is important that the director is highly organised and has a clear idea of how they are going to bring the script to life. Preparing storyboards can help the director work out complicated sequences. Directors need to be good communicators to instruct the cast and crew. In a multi-camera studio environment the director will sit in the gallery and call the shots, and relay information to the camera operators and studio floor via a talkback system. If the programme is pre-recorded the director will be involved in the post-production phase, working with the editor. In a single-camera drama the director is more likely to be on the studio floor. Jet Wilkinson gives this insight into the busy schedule of a studio TV drama director:

> As a director on a continuing drama generally you would be booked for a five-week contract where you read the scripts and then you have a week and [a] half of preparation on the scripts when you talk about the scripts in the script department, make changes, make your notes, then you talk about it with the crew and set it all up, talk about costuming, props, locations, and you organise the shoot with your first ADs and the crew and then you shoot location for anywhere up to three to four, maybe five days and then in studio for any length of time for up to seven days, and then you edit about three or four days. It's a very quick turnaround and you have to achieve a lot in a short amount of time.

Production Manager (PM)

The PM is responsible for logistics and making sure everything is happening on budget and on schedule. If a PM is overseeing responsibility for more than one production they are typically referred to as a Unit Manager. See Chapter 5 for further details on this role.

Production Co-ordinator and Production Secretary

These roles provide back-up logistical support to the PM. You need to be highly organised to take on these job roles. They involve compiling the call sheets, booking the studio, transport, accommodation, crew and equipment. Typically someone might start as a Production Secretary, then move up to Production Co-ordinator and then PM level.

Assistant Producer (AP)

The AP provides essential support editorially and logistically to the producer. APs are responsible for setting up and researching stories, liaising with talent and contributors, checking content of scripts, briefing the presenter and guests with the producer, and helping to organise and schedule shoots.

Researcher

Researchers work with the APs to find stories and contributors, and check facts. They may take on the role of celebrity booker on a talk or chat show and be involved in preparing briefing notes and question-wrangling on game shows (writing quiz questions). They ensure the presenter and guests are happy and get release forms signed. Typically a researcher moves up to AP level and then becomes a producer or director or both, referred to as a PD, a role that is most commonly seen on factual shows.

Runner

This is the entry-level position for most people starting out in the industry. It is a useful place to start as it gives you the opportunity to see how everything works. Your tasks may seem pretty menial and involve photocopying scripts and making tea, but try to remember you will not be a runner forever and smile! Keep looking for chances to help out that go beyond your role – word will quickly get around that you are talented and hard-working. It is also extremely useful to have a driving licence so that you can run errands and ferry the talent around. Having this on your CV will help you get your foot in the door.

On large-scale shows there will be more than one producer, AP, researcher and runner.

Gallery Production Assistant/Script Supervisor

The PA or script supervisor sits next to the director in the gallery and is different to a drama supervisor, who checks continuity, ensuring there are no errors in set, costume or dialogue, necessary as drama is rarely shot in chronological order. A gallery PA, however, provides countdowns and makes sure the final show comes out at the required length.

Katherine Morgan (*Match of the Day, Mastermind*) explains what her job as a live gallery PA entails:

> The director will have prepared the running order and then the PA works with the director to produce the camera cards which break down each item and give shot information for the camera operators. It's the PA's job to assist the director by giving counts on each item, saying how long is left and what item is coming next to ensure that the director can get all the shots in the allocated time. A PA will shot call the next item and run the VTs. Quite often a PA will go on to be a director.

Scriptwriters and Script Editors

Depending on the genre there will be a designated scriptwriter or scriptwriters. On a soap or sitcom in the UK they typically each take responsibility for a single show. On factual and entertainment programmes the job of writing the script often falls to the producer or director. Script editors are invaluable on big long-running series. They oversee the scripts, checking their feasibility, and provide a link between the production team and the writers. Scriptwriter Sam Snape, with TV credits on *All Creatures Great and Small, Soldier Soldier* and *Casualty* offers these tips for budding writers:

> It is essential to watch the shows you want to write for. If you aspire you need to admire. Your need for self-expression as a writer comes second to the show's need to speak to its audience. Soaps and sitcoms are the staple food of TV so must reflect society as it is being lived. It's good to observe and understand how real people live and work. So,

when you come to write the enhanced realism that is soap or sitcom, you will write with empathy about the inevitable flaws of the characters. Make us laugh. Make us think. Above all, make us care!

Floor Manager (FM) and Assistant Floor Manager (AFM)

The FM is in charge of the studio floor and relays instructions from the director via talkback to the crew, cast and guests. They use a system of hand signals to cue the talent as to what camera they are on and how much time they have on an item. The FM ensures that health and safety procedures are adhered to and that any props required are brought onto the set at the correct time. Anything that happens on the studio floor must go through the FM. An AFM assists the floor manager on big productions.

First Assistant Director/Second Assistant Director

The first AD or second AD are job roles most commonly found in drama. They assist the director in a similar way to an FM and ensure the smooth running of the show. They also provide a link between the director, cast, crew and production team.

They are responsible for ensuring health and safety rules are followed and that there are no delays to the schedule or the budget!

Lighting Director

The lighting director sits in the gallery during the shoot and is in charge of all aspects of lighting. They work closely with the director to bring the script to life by designing a lighting plan for the show. On big shows with complicated lighting set-ups they might be joined by a team including a gaffer (head electrician) and best boy (assistant).

Vision Mixer

The vision mixer sits to the right of the director in the gallery and cuts the programme live. They have to be in sync with the director, listening carefully to their instructions. They have a number of transitions to choose from; in most cases a traditional cut or wipe will be used but on modern vision mixers there are any number of weird and wonderful options to choose from! From the bank of monitors they can cut to VTs (video tape) or graphics. Often vision mixers go on to become directors and, on short, uncomplicated or low-budget programmes, the director often doubles up as the vision mixer.

Technical Manager/Vision Engineer

The TM or TD (technical director) checks that all equipment is working and, when the lights are in place for the show, the TM can adjust the camera settings accordingly. The TM helps the director with any technical knowledge, taking responsibility for colour balance and picture quality and ensures the programme is aired to broadcast quality.

Director of Photography (DOP), Camera Supervisor and Camera Operators

The DOP, in drama and factual, and the camera supervisor, in multicamera studio set-ups, is in charge of the camera team. A DOP/camera supervisor works with the director to realise their vision. They help the director with the blocking during the rehearsal stage, planning where the camera needs to be. They must be creatively and technically adept. The camera operators frame the shots and operate the camera, panning, tilting and zooming as instructed by the director via talkback. The camera team may also require a jib operator and assistant jib operator for sweeping shots. Simon Reay talks about the difference between a camera operator and a DOP:

> Director of photography is often used as a sort of grander camera operator, but the term itself is the reason that I do what I do. I engage with the script and with the director and listen to what actually needs to happen on screen and interpret that visually. So where the camera placement is, where the camera is, where the audience is, what their perspective is, and that is what a DOP is, in my mind.

Sound

Sound supervisors are in charge of the sound quality. They need to microphone (mic) the contributors and talent and check sound levels to ensure clarity. It is a good idea to ask an open-ended question while you are testing the levels so that you have time to get this right, such as 'tell me how you got to the studio?' or 'what did you eat for lunch?' On a live multi-camera show a sound supervisor monitors sound output and ensures it is high quality. They may have a sound assistant on a big show.

VT Operator/EVS Operator

The VT operator is responsible for adding in any VTs or assets. These include graphics, Astons (name captions), title sequences or location-based pre-recorded VTs (short films). EVS is a digital media company that started in 1994 and specialises in live digital recording for broadcasting. An EVS operator works on live entertainment and sports shows with the capacity to create live replays.

Grams

The grams operator sits in the gallery and plays in live jingles, music, titles and sound effects.

Autocue

The autocue operator, sometimes referred to as the teleprompt, sits in the gallery and is in charge of the speed at which the script appears on the camera for the presenter to read – it is important to practise this in rehearsal so that you go at the right pace for the presenter. If any changes are made to the script it is the autocue operator's responsibility to make these changes.

Art Department

The production designer is in charge of the art department. They take overall responsibility for designing and delivering the director's vision for the show. Other members of the art team include the set designer and art director, who assist the production designer with creating the look and build of the set and work closely with the director and producer. Other people in the art team on a big studio show include the production buyer, who sources and buys any required props, and the property (props) master, who is responsible for looking after all the props on the set.

Make-up and Costume

Don't underestimate these roles. Having the appropriate make-up and costume for talent and contributors can help with confidence and avoid shiny faces under the hot studio lights! Presenters often have a costume budget and a favourite stylist to source suitable outfits for them to wear. It is important that everyone appearing on-screen wears appropriate clothing; so no offensive logos, as this will cause compliance issues, and no noisy rustling clothes or jewellery that jangles and interferes with the microphones. Also it is important to avoid any overly patterned clothing such as small checks or stripes that can cause the cameras to strobe. On big studio drama productions the costume department can have an entire warehouse full of clothes, bags, hats and shoes to choose from, and have to work with the director and producer to source costumes for the whole cast, in keeping with their character.

Cable Basher

This is a junior job but still a very important one. The studio TV cameras have long cables and it is the job of the cable basher to assist the camera operators, ensuring that they can move smoothly and swiftly around the studio without getting tangled in the cables.

Warm-up Artist

Studio shows with a live audience generally have a warm-up artist to entertain the audience in between the long takes if pre-recorded and during any commercial breaks. The warm-up artist motions to the audience when to clap, remain quiet or laugh. They typically provide the audience with a health and safety briefing before the start of the show.

Conclusion

For individuals interested in pursuing a career in the television industry, there are a number of different routes into the TV industry and a huge selection of jobs available which require talented, enthusiastic people. For all the information on routes in and career options, look at: http://creativeskillset.org/creative_industries/tv/ways_into_the_industry

Now Back to the Studio

The studio gallery

The gallery, or control room, is essentially a small but incredibly important room where all the controls are. Typically it is next to the studio or above it via a flight of stairs. On some gallery set-ups the gallery area is split, with a separate room for sound control and maybe a separate room for graphics, EVS operator and VT operator. All communication in and out of the gallery is via a telecoms talk-back system and there are strict etiquette protocols that should be adhered to at all times. The gallery is very much the domain of the studio director. It is only the director who speaks to the floor manager to convey messages to the studio floor, and the only voices heard during a recording should be that of the director, production assistant and producer. Katherine Morgan explains why:

> You need to be as quiet as possible as quite often the talkback will be 'open' to the presenter (which means they can hear everything in the gallery) and this is very off-putting to the presenter who is listening to the director and the PA giving them directions.

Examples of director commands

▸ Good luck everyone (it's important to motivate your team);
▸ Lights up;
▸ We are recording;
▸ Roll titles (start the title sequence);
▸ Cue/roll Aston/wipe Aston (Aston, as we've said, refers to name or place text that appears at the bottom of the screen, sometimes referred to as a 'cap gen' (CG), 'caption generator' or a 'name super', as it is a superimposed image;
▸ Cue presenter, for example 'Cue Claudia' so that she begins talking;
▸ Cue applause, cut applause (this could be a live audience or a soundtrack);
▸ Wipe screen (to get rid of an image on the screen);
▸ To camera ops: standby 2 – go 2, standby 1 – go 1, or the director might say ready 2 – take 2 – ready 3 – take 3 – ready 1 – take 1 etc. (standby/ready warns the camera operator that they are going to take their shot and a tally light then appears on the camera that is being used;

- Standby VT/roll VT/lose VT
- Pan left/right, track (dolly) in/out, tilt up/down, crab left/right, centre/up, zoom in/out.;
- Fade to black (end of show);
- Well done everyone. End on a positive note and show your respect for your team.

Examples of what a PA says in the gallery

The script supervisor (PA) sits to the left of the director and typically says the following:

- Standby/silence in gallery or standby/silence on studio floor;
- Counts into the programme/in and out of VTs;
- Twenty seconds to titles/twenty seconds left on titles, then ten seconds etc.;
- Recording/Live in 10, 9, 8, 7, 6, 5, 4, 3, 2, 1, 0;
- Coming to break – it's very important you do not 'fall off air';
- Time each part – one minute gone etc.

Only a select few members of the production team and crew get to enter the gallery. Below is a list of the jobs that you would usually expect to see in a gallery during the recording of a show (any additional people wanting to enter the gallery would need to get approval from the director or producer):

- Executive producer;
- Programme editor;
- Producer;
- Director;
- Vision mixer;
- Gallery production assistant/script supervisor;
- Lighting director;
- Technical director;
- Sound supervisor;
- Grams operator;
- VT operator/EVS operator;
- Autocue operator.

You should familiarise yourself with the rules that govern the studio environment, such as no eating or drinking (exceptions are water for the presenter or contributors, or for a food programme!) and noise must be kept to a minimum. The studio and gallery doors

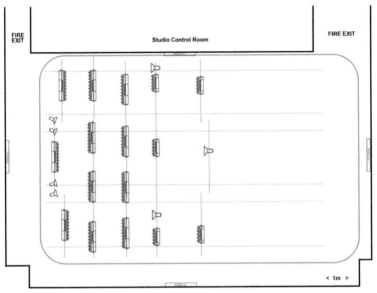

Image 4 Lighting plan

should remain closed at all times to reduce noise. A red light appears outside the studio if there is a recording in progress – never enter at this time or you will face the wrath of the whole production!

Getting ready to shoot in a studio

Getting ready to shoot in a studio requires a lot of preparation and a lot of paperwork. The PM, along with the team, will prepare a master call sheet for the studio day, including camera scripts, running orders and overall schedule for the day (see Chapter 5 for full details). Departments will also have started preparing for the show in advance, such as the lighting department and graphics team. The studio you are using will provide you with a floor and lighting plan, and then you can start to think about the scale of the show and where the set and cameras will go.

Running order

The running order lists all items and their duration. The running order is particularly important in factual, entertainment and news shows, especially if the programme is live as you won't have another opportunity to re-shoot – if you go over the show's agreed running time you will end up falling off air! The director will typically compile the running order with the help of the PA. A useful rule to remember when doing your timings is that three words are roughly equal to a second of air time.

Sample running order

Item	Description	Presenter	Guests	Running Time (R/T)	Duration	Source (V/T/Caption/Graphics, Props etc.)
1	PRESENTER INTRO & MENU	Bob	Kate X Richard X	00:45:00	00:00:45	Caption menu
2	INTRO PANEL	Bob	Kate X Richard X	00:01:15	00:00:30	Caption guests/anything they're promoting, e.g. book/CD
2	MAIN TOPIC PANEL DISCUSSION	–	XXX XXX	00:03:30	00:02:15	Caption topic headline/newspaper clip
3	LINK TO VOX POPS	XXX	N/A	00:03:45	00:00:15	–
4	VOX POPS	Roving reporter Neil	Vox pops	00:04:30	00:00:45	V/T
5	OUTLINK – TOPIC 2	XXX	XXX XXX	00:05:55	00:01:25	–
6	GOODBYES AND BRIEF TRAIL FOR TOMORROW'S SHOW	XXX	XXX XXX	00:06:40	00:00:45	–
7	END CREDITS	–	–	00:07:00	00:00:20	Graphics

Everything is timed to the second to ensure all air time is filled and crucial timings (for commercial breaks etc.) are all met.

Camera script

In a multi-camera environment, the cameras are given numbers from one upwards. The camera script typically includes a list of all the cameras and what shots the director wants them to get. The director then marks up technical camera directions on the left-hand side of the page. The words spoken by the cast, presenters and contributors appear on the right-hand side, along with any technical instructions about which source the sound is coming from, for example SOT (Sound On Tape). See the script extracts in Chapters 6–13 to look at the different layouts and how they vary from genre to genre. You will typically see a list of cameras on the front page of a camera script:

Camera 1: Singles on guests 'as directed'
Camera 2: 3S guests (three shot)
Camera 3: MS presenter (mid shot) or 4S (four shot)
Camera 4: MCU guests (medium close-up) or MCU presenter
Camera 5: WS (wide shots) opening and closing moves

Shot list and camera cards

The director needs to prepare a detailed shot list. Preparation is key for a smooth-running show and most of this prep happens well before the day of the shoot. The shot list is then broken down and each camera operator is provided with a camera card that they can attach to their camera so they know the shots that they are required to get. The director, with the help of the PA, compiles the camera cards. You may see the words 'as directed' on the script for unscripted shows, and this requires the camera operators to follow the conversation of a guest or contributor 'on the fly' – they will have been given a number of shots to get and will need to use their initiative in framing shots and listen carefully to the director's instructions through talkback.

Sample shot list

Shot No	Cam No.	Shot Description	Script	Duration
1	2	Presenter PTC	You can include the in and out here – for example 'Hello and welcome to today's show ...... coming up we are joined by our film reviewers'	30"

Shot No	Cam No.	Shot Description	Script	Duration
2	1	2S guests	'Sandy and Sam' Hellos	10"
3	3	WS	Now over to ...	5"
4	1	As directed	Interview with Sandy and Sam	–

Sample camera card

Cam 1		
Shot No	Description of Shot	Duration
1	MS	10"
4	MCU	5"
6	2S	5"

Studio camera moves and shot sizes

It's important to be up to speed with the terminology and grammar of TV and the shots used. Here are just a few basic terms to get you started:

- **Zoom in/out:** Adjusting the zoom lens (not the camera) so that you are closer or further away from the action/cast;
- **Tilt up/down:** Moving the head of the camera up or down;
- **Pedestal (ped) up/down:** Moving the height of the camera up or down;
- **Pan right/left:** Turning the lens to the right or left;
- **Dolly in/out:** Moving with the camera forward or backward;
- **Truck left/right:** Moving with the camera to the left or right;
- **1S/2S/3S:** One shot/two shot etc. refers to the number of people in the camera frame;
- **WS/MS/MCU/CU/ECU:** Wide shot, mid shot, medium close-up, close-up, extreme close-up – indicate the shot size the director wants;
- **Pick ups:** Retakes of any additional sequences. On a pre-recorded show, notes are taken of any mistakes, such as a presenter fluffing their line or a sitcom not getting the intended laugh, and then typically all are re-shot at the end of the studio day.

Talent and contributors

When you are inviting guests to the studio, whether it's for an audition, rehearsal or recording, it's important that you behave professionally and look after them. Here are a few top tips from us on what to think about so that you will get the best performances possible and everyone will have a great shoot!

‣ Assign a member of the team to look after talent/guests;
‣ Provide regular refreshments. It's hard to perform if you are thirsty or hungry;
‣ Be encouraging and positive;
‣ Brief them thoroughly so that they feel prepared and are clear about what you want;
‣ Keep to time.

Now Try This

1. Draw up a schedule and running order for your show. Remember you need to keep to time. You cannot afford to over-run in the studio!
2. Book tickets for a studio show. While you're there, look carefully at the studio environment. How many cameras are they using? How many crew are there on the studio floor? Did anything surprise you? Would you do anything differently?
3. Source a sofa (try your student union), a lamp and two flats. Buy some wallpaper to decorate the flats and dress your set. Work with the lighting director and art team to work out a colour scheme. Think about whether you will have an audience and whether you will break the fourth wall, as they do in *Miranda*, *Peep Show* and *Mrs Brown's Boys* by talking directly to the viewer at home. There are so many possibilities – be creative!

5

PRODUCTION MANAGEMENT

Congratulations, your idea has been greenlit! Now the work begins as you enter the pre-production stage. Pre-production is when the idea comes to life and the planning of your idea begins. The production manager is key in managing the logistics, and in drawing up a budget and schedule so that the production team have a clear framework to use.

Here we will look at:

▸ The role of a production manager;
▸ Budget and schedules;
▸ Clearances and delivery requirements.

Remember there are three stages of production (and four if you count development):

▸ **Stage One:** Idea development and winning a commission, which is usually led by the executive producer
▸ **Stage Two:** Pre-production
▸ **Stage Three:** Production – this is when filming begins
▸ **Stage Four:** Post-production – this is the editing process

The pre-production stage is spearheaded by the production manager, who has the job of getting the right people, meaning the cast and crew, in the right place, whether that be on location or in the studio, on schedule and within budget. Creative Skillset (www.creativeskillset.org) provides a comprehensive look at the role of the production manager and the skills required for this pivotal production role. In essence, production managers help to determine the most efficient and cost-effective way to schedule shoots, negotiate deals and make day-to-day production decisions to ensure the production runs smoothly.

In pre-production, production managers work closely with the producer and, if it is a drama, also with the first assistant director to break down the script page by page and to develop a provisional schedule. They then consult with the various heads of department to estimate the materials needed and begin a draft budget. Once the overall budget has been signed off, production managers assist producers in selecting crews and suppliers. They also oversee the search for locations and liaise with local authorities and the police regarding permits and other permissions.

During production, production managers ensure that all invoices are paid and help the production accountant prepare weekly cost reports. They also oversee production paperwork, such as release forms, call sheets and daily progress reports. They make changes to the schedule and to the budget as required, and ensure that these changes are brought to the attention of all relevant personnel. Production managers deal with any personnel problems or issues that may arise, and ensure that all health and safety regulations are adhered to.

Production managers need to be aware of compliance issues and Ofcom regulations. Ofcom is the government-approved regulatory and competition authority for the media and telecoms sectors. One of its roles is to protect the public from harmful or offensive material. Viewers may contact Ofcom to complain about the time of day a programme is screened, unfair treatment of contributors or factual inaccuracies to name some. More details can be found on their website: www.ofcom.org.uk

Risk Assessments

If you are working in the studio, usually a master risk assessment form has been completed by your head of studios; unless you are doing anything out of the ordinary you may not need to complete these each time. However, if you are filming VTs, which are short films, on location you will need a separate risk assessment form for each shoot. You will also often be asked for a copy of your organisation's public liability insurance to gain permission for certain locations.

Here's an extract from a risk assessment form – every company and organisation will have their own version which is updated regularly to reflect changing health and safety regulations. As you will see it is a series of tick boxes to work through, rating the severity of each risk. This is then followed by more detailed analysis for any risks identified, complete with plans of what you will do to ensure safety and limit these risks.

Extract from a risk assessment form

No	Hazard	No	Hazard	No	Hazard
01	Access/egress blocked/restricted	14	First aid/medical requirements	27	Noise/high sound levels
02	Alcoholic drinks	15	Flammable materials: painting/spraying	28	Portable tools above 110v
03	Animals/insects	16	Flying/aircraft/balloons/parachutes	29	Psychological/physiological/physical exertion/stress
04	Any specialist prop under the direct control of the presenter/artist	17	Hazardous substances: chemicals/dust/fumes/poisons/asbestos/battery acid	30	Radiation sources/equipment
05	Audience safety/public/crowds	18	Waste disposal	31	Risk of infection
06	Compressed gas/cryogenics/low temperatures	19	Heat/cold, extreme weather/climate	32	Scaffolds/rostra/decking/platforms/practical staircase/walkways on set
07	Confined space/tanks/mines/caves/tunnels	20	Heavy loads on location/set floor/rostra	33	Scenery/flats
08	Derelict buildings/dangerous structures/isolation of services	21	LPG/bottled gases	34	Scenic/set materials – not fire retardant
09	Diving operations	22	Lasers/other bright lights/strobes	35	Scenery, manual handling difficulties
10	Explosives/pyrotechnics/fireworks	23	Lifting equipment e.g. forklift	36	Scenic materials: glass/polystyrene
11	Falling objects	24	Live electrical equipment	37	Smoking on set
12	Fatigue/long hours	25	Machinery proximity	38	Special rigs
13	Fire prevention/evacuation	26	Night operations	39	Special needs/children/elderly/disabled

No	Hazard	No	Hazard	No	Hazard
40	Special visual effects: rain/snow/fire/smoke/steam/dry ice/heat	45	Water/proximity to water/tank	50	Other (detail)
41	Scenery/props/storage on premises	46	Weapons/knives/firearms	51	–
42	Stunts/dangerous activities/hazardous props	47	Working at height/ladders/scaffold	52	–
43	Camera crane/jib/dolly/camera cables/camera movement/special cable runs	48	Working on grid	53	–
44	Vehicles/motorcycles/speed	49	Working/storage under seating	54	–

Probability and severity calculator

Severity / Probability	Minor Injury	Lost Time/ Ill Health	Major Injury	Permanent Disability	Fatal
Highly unlikely	1	2	3	4	5
Unlikely	2	4	6	8	10
Possible	3	6	9	12	15
Probable	4	8	12	16	20
Certain	5	10	15	20	25

For each of the risks you identify you will rate the probability of the event happening, along with the severity factor. This is all about demonstrating duty of care and carefully considering in advance what you need to do to safely achieve your filming goals. Remember should something go wrong this documentation will be referred back to so it is important you get this right, and even more important is that if you say you are going to do something, for example, wearing high-visibility jackets for a night shoot, you actually follow these instructions.

Matthew Welch, head of studios and a programme-maker, has some good examples of what not to do!

> We had an instance of a crew filming a chase sequence with guns in a park, but they failed to inform the police and ended up being

arrested with a full complement of two helicopters, tactical gun units, and tens of squad cars! Not an easy situation to talk yourself out of!

I have also had to replace an entire studio floor once because lights were taken off stands before properly cooled and they melted the floor!

Know How Your Production Works

It is important to understand the requirements of your production. How will the researchers generate stories and contestants? What's your programme's policy on paying guests? How will you source-check your stories and contributors to make sure they are who they say they are? How will you find the graphics to explain a difficult news item or act out a difficult scene?

Checking a contributor's identification is a basic requirement and good journalistic practice. In factual-based shows that use members of the public, make sure to check the contributor's passport or a photo driver's licence, plus perhaps ask for two further sources of identification like utility bills. Double-check stories by asking to speak to those that can corroborate the story such as a boss, a mother, friend etc.

When hiring actors it is good to be aware of Equity, which is the British actors' union. Andrew Parker, actor and lecturer says:

> The guidelines take a realistic approach to student budgets – simply suggesting that actors should not accept payment below the hourly rate set out by the National Minimum Wage. Choosing an actor who is a member of Equity should bring certain advantages to the production. A professional actor brings their craft and discipline to your film in the same way as the director or editor does. They are a core part of your team, and should have the appropriate mind-set. To join the union, an actor must provide contractual or financial evidence of paid acting work. In other words, union membership is proof of some relevant experience.
>
> But beware – there are many excellent, new actors who do not yet have Equity membership or agency representation! You may see them in other student films, or in unpaid fringe theatre shows, and they may be perfect for you. Whomever you cast you will have to convince them of your own professionalism, and of the integrity of your production. They will want to collaborate with you if you can produce the same quality of work in your area of expertise as they can in theirs.

Production schedule

The production schedule is the glue that holds your production together. The overall master schedule will contain information on team start dates, delivery dates, key deadlines, TX (transmission) dates etc. Remember if you are being funded by a broadcaster to check the commissioning editor's availability – if they are away on holiday for the whole of August you may have a backlog in the edit suite that will hamper your schedule and delay your production. Use your delivery date and work backwards to work out the production run length. So if it's January now and you have to deliver this series by June of the same year, you have 6 months or 24 weeks to play with. This then gives you the building blocks to know you will require a production manager for 24 weeks, a part-time exec for 12 weeks etc. Create a simple Excel spreadsheet to plot the key dates for your programme.

Example master production schedule
XXX Productions
1 x 60" Broadcaster

	Wk 1	Wk 2	Wk 3	Wk 4	Wk 5
Research/casting/location finding	Start				
Sign off: Vets/contributor stories/location		Due for completion			
B/story filming			Start filming		
Studio + 4 wk treatment period					Begin studio
Offline				Offline inserts	
Post-production and master delivery					
Clear up					
Exec viewings/legal compliance					
Production Personnel:					
Executive Producer	Start date				
Producer/Director	Start date				

	Wk 1	**Wk 2**	**Wk 3**	**Wk 4**	**Wk 5**
Production Manager	Start date				
Shooting AP		Start date			
Casting Researcher	Start date				
Production Co-ordinator: 15 wks over period	Start date				
Presenter: Jo Page					
Vet Presenter					
Runner			Start date		
Stylist: Set				Start date	

Budgeting

So now we have a rough idea of the schedule we can start working out the budget. Budgets are often referred to as having three sections: 'above the line', 'below the line' and 'indirect costs'. Above the line can include the costs for the script, director, producer and actors. This is particularly important when working on big feature films when you are trying to secure A-list Hollywood stars that command multimillion-pound fees. We tend to not include your 'everyday' director and actor costs in this line. Below the line costs include cast, crew and equipment. These figures alter slightly as pre-production begins. Indirect costs are items like office overheads which are ongoing business costs.

If you are creating a brand-new budget for your studio show, what follows below is a list of the industry standard schedule items that production companies and broadcasters use to track costs. This includes everything from cameras through to location costs. While at university you do not need to worry about things like overheads as you will be using the course's resources, but it is good to begin to understand how this works. There are some software packages available to help you budget but all you need is a spreadsheet package and you can devise your own.

When beginning your budget, work in broad figures to speed up the process. You initially want a feel for the numbers to see how it is working. Then go back and revise with more accurate figures, searching for the best deals. It will take a few drafts before you get it right. When you begin to think about budgeting ensure you are clear about the duration of the programme, the technical delivery requirements and the clearances required. Crucially, make sure you know the delivery date as everything revolves around this.

Here are the typical items you will find in a budget, usually in this order, standardising it in this way makes it easy for those involved in production finance to locate budget lines.

Example budget items

Item	Description (these can be added to)
Development, Story, Script	• Agreed development costs • Rights • Writers' fees
Producer/Director	• Executive producer • Series producer • Producer • Director • Associate producer
Artistes	• Actors
Presenters, Interviewees	• Presenter • Voice-over • Contributors
Production Unit Salaries	• Production manager • Production co-ordinator • Production accountant • Production secretary • Researcher
Assistant Directors, Continuity	• Assistant directors • Script supervisors
Crew – Camera	• DOP • Camera operator
Crew – Sound	• Sound recordist
Crew – Lighting	• Lighting director • Electrician
Crew – Art Department	• Set designer • Prop buyer • Graphic designer
Crew – Wardrobe, Make-up, Hair	• Costume designer • Make-up supervisor
Crew – Editing	• Editor • Dubbing mixer

Item	Description (these can be added to)
Crew – 2nd Unit	• 2nd Unit
Wage-related Overheads	• Employer's national insurance contributions etc.
Materials – Art Department	• Set • Props
Materials – Wardrobe, Make-up, Hair	• Costumes • Make-up stock
Production Equipment	• Camera and sound hire • Consumables
Facility Package Arrangements	• Block deals for crew, for example, camera and sound operator with kit
Studio, OBs	• Studio hire • Outside broadcast hire
Other Production Facilities	• Location fees • Location equipment
Stock/Hard Drives	• Hard drives
Post-production	• All post-production costs
Archive, Stills	• Royalties • Stills
Rostrum, Graphics	• Title sequences • Rostrum hire
Music	• Composer • Sync rights
Travel, Transport	• Car hire • Taxis • Excess baggage
Hotel, Living	• Accommodation • Hospitality and subsistence
Other Production Costs	• Transcripts • Research materials • Visas
Insurance, Finance, Legal	• Insurance • Legal fees
Production Overheads	• Office rent • IT and phones

BECTU, the Broadcasting, Entertainment, Cinematograph and Theatre Union, has some useful resources to help with production management, including rate cards so you can work out typical crew fees. Phone up facility houses and ask what they would charge for equipment and resources. Remember there are always deals to be done!

Student Project Budget

For student-based studio entertainment projects you are probably most concerned with budget lines:

- Presenter and contributor fees;
- Travel, transport;
- Hotel, living;
- Other production costs.

Devise a simple spreadsheet or table to keep across costs. It can be stressful when you are funding your own projects and need to divide expenses between you. Planning, agreeing and tracking costs will help. First set a budget and all contribute your share upfront. Make sure the producer tracks costs. If you are going over budget this needs to be quickly agreed and you need to decide upon how this will be funded, just as you would in a real-world production.

Item	Estimated Cost	Final Cost	Difference
Presenter Fees	£100	£100	£0
Travel to London	4 × train fares to London @ £16 each = £64	8 × train fares as needed an extra filming day = £128	£64

Schedule

While you have a master schedule for the overall production plan you will also need a detailed schedule for the individual filming days. A typical studio day is 10–12 hours and people are called to the studio at different times depending on their job role. Usually the day begins with a production meeting, followed by a thorough camera rehearsal to allow the director to block through the programme with the camera operators. Camera scripts are updated after rehearsals and printed on a new colour to avoid any mix-ups.

Example schedule: pre-recorded studio entertainment show

Time	Schedule	
Date		
07h30	Call time for rigging jib	
08h00	Call time for Production	

Time	Schedule	
Date		
08h30	Call time for guests to make-up/wardrobe and briefing Call time for Crew	
09h15	Call time for Cast	
09h30–10h00	Camera rehearsal	
10h00	RX as directed	
12h00	Call time for SFX	
13h00	Lunch Call time for (Autocue)	
14h00	RX as directed	
19h30	Wrap	
	Strike	

When creating a schedule it is very important to be clear about working hours and ensure that crew, production and actors are all getting breaks that follow health and safety law. If you are working with children you may need a performance licence for them. Details for these can be found on LEA (Local Education Authority) websites – it is always important to check as rules can change from year to year. There are strict rules about working hours for children – usually a maximum of six hours and requirement of a parent, guardian or chaperone to be in attendance at all times. You may also need the production team and crew to have a DBS (Disclosure and Barring Service) check if working with children. This was formerly known as a CRB check (Criminal Records Bureau). If you are in any doubt, discuss with your tutor/executive producer. Remember, though, you will need parental consent for anyone under 18 to appear in your programme.

When creating your daily schedule don't forget about catering. A fed crew will be a happy crew! If you have not planned where you will be eating then time can be wasted looking for somewhere. Also decide in advance if you are paying for catering or not. Let your teams know so they too can plan. Sometimes laying on catering, while there is a cost to your budget, can save you time and money, ensuring the crew are ready to start again at the scheduled time.

Call Sheets

Call sheets, as the name suggests, provide all of the detail a crew and production need to arrive on a shoot or studio record on time in the right place and be prepared for the day. Here is a sample version that you can adapt for either studio or location to create your own version:

Sample studio call sheet

Title of programme:
Production office address and phone number:
Date/time of studio record/shoot:
Location of shoot:
Weather and daylight hours if filming on location:

Contributor/Actor Details	Name	Contact Details	
Production Contacts * add as required			
Job Title	Name	Email	Tel No
Exec Producer			
Series Producer			
Producer			
Director			
Production Manager			
Assistant Producer			
Script Supervisor			
Researcher			
Runner			
Studio/Crew Contacts * add as required			
Floor Manager			
Assistant Floor Manager			
Lighting Director			
Vision Mixer			
Camera Supervisor			
Jib Operator			
Jib Assistant			
Camera			

Sound Supervisor			
Sound Operator			
Autocue Operator			
Hair Designer			
Make-up Designer			
Costume Designer			
Set Designer			

Equipment and Technical Requirements

List all kit requirements – camera, lights, sound, batteries etc. for location shoots

Travel *inc as appropriate

Taxi details

Vehicle hire details

Train/flight details

Parking details

Accommodation

Hotel details

Health and Safety

Insurance details

Local hospital

Local police station

Local authority details

Other Useful Information

Map of location and directions

Full risk assessment

Release forms to be signed

Keep receipts

Schedule Example	
09h00	Production and crew call
	Crew brief
09h45	Tech check
	Talent call time
	Editorial team: brief talent/guests

10h30	Rehearsal
	Block-through to plan camera positions/ mark presenter or cast positions
	Stagger-through – stop and start until everyone is happy with what they are doing
	Run-through rehearsal (often recorded as safety net)
12h00	Break for lunch
13h00	Record (RX)
17h30	Strike set
18h00	Wrap

Call sheets for a long-running series like *Coronation Street* will be sent out weekly and updated daily, by the production co-ordinators and managers, to reflect what has been accomplished during the filming day. There is little opportunity to over-run as they are working close to transmission deadlines.

Here is a an example of a call sheet adapted from *Coronation Street*:

Example call sheet: *Coronation Street*

CORONATION STREET REHEARSAL SCRIPT 8660
WRITER: xxx
DIRECTOR: xxx
TRANSMISSION: xxx
EPISODE: 5 (of 5) Story Day 3 = Friday
PRODUCTION WEEKS:
SHOOTING DATES:
RECORDING SUNRISE/SUNSET:
TRANSMISSION SUNRISE/SUNSET:
NB Please refer to 1st AD's Shooting Schedule & Daily Call Sheets for full details of shooting hours, calls & locations
CAST LIST
xxx
PRODUCTION TEAM
xxx
Press Office: xxx
Running Order
Programme Name: Coronation Street
Programme ID:
Episode Number:

SC	SET	PAGES	DAY/TIME	STUDIO	LOCATION
1	INT No.8	(1–3)	Day 3	Callum	
	Platts (ST4)		15:01	David	
				Kylie	
				Gail	
				Sarah	

David announces to an incredulous Callum and Sarah that he and Kylie are giving it another go. Gail comes in and eyes Kylie contemptuously. A gleeful Callum sits, ready to watch Gail unload on Kylie.

Clearances

Clearances are essential to complete for your programmes. If you do not get them completed properly you will not be able to enter your films into festivals or broadcast them. Clearance forms are needed for contributors, locations and any still image or archive footage used. Where possible, clear everything for worldwide rights. With the rise of the internet and the re-versioning of material, it is wise to clear everything for use in all forms so you are future-proofed. Your university or company will have their own templates to use.

Within your programme you are likely to want to use music for opening titles, stings and to create changes of mood. Sometimes for copyright reasons it is easier to get music specially composed (if you can, do a buy-out deal) for your show so you are free to use it as you wish within the programme. There are also copyright-free music tracks available. Explore if there is a music course in your university that you can collaborate with. If you do not clear your music properly this could limit you entering your programmes into festivals or getting broadcast, so it is important to do it properly.

When adding music to programmes there are commonly three areas to consider licensing in order to ensure your work is fully cleared; these are mechanical, performance and master rights of music held by music writers, artists, publishers and record labels. The effective licensing of these three forms of copyright ensures the rightholders get recompensed in royalties for the use of their work. The Performance Rights Society (www.prsmusic.com) is worth exploring for more information. It can be a complex process, so it's worth seeking advice.

Delivery

When you are delivering your programme to either a broadcaster, festival or for your course assignment, they will want to know everything has been cleared correctly so as not to infringe any copyright issues. Be careful of background music, which you may have not noticed playing when you were filming, or photos on display behind a contributor – if they are in shot or can be heard at all they will need to be cleared. The photo may have been taken by a professional wedding photographer, for example, who will own the actual copyright. All of the paperwork relating to the programme needs to be passed to the broadcaster or funder to demonstrate all is in order; this includes music cue sheets, release forms, location agreements, stills agreements etc.

Multiplatform

Do not forget to include multiplatform content planning into your production schedule. Behind-the-scenes material can help build an audience for your show, but someone needs to be getting these things prepared. Social media activity and teasing clips on YouTube can all help build your audience. The documentary film made by University of Hertfordshire students, *A Boy and his Dog*, achieved 4.5 million hits and rising on YouTube, which created a buzz for their production and media interest.

Summary

The production manager's role includes:

▸ Budgeting;
▸ Scheduling;
▸ Awareness of industry regulations and health and safety policy;
▸ Preparation, preparation, preparation!

Remember, if you are not sure about something then ask. It can be difficult when you first start out and feel like you are asking questions constantly, but it is best to get it right or it can have serious repercussions. Make sure you are adhering to good practice and all health and safety considerations.

Now Try This

Try out these production management scenarios and devise some solutions. What would you do?

1. Your presenter or actor is coming to set late, which is causing your budget and schedule to over-run. As a production manager, what kinds of things could you do to ease this? Think about organising transport for the presenter to collect them from home so you can control their movement – what else could you do?
2. Select a piece of commercial music and investigate how you would go about clearing it.
3. Have a go at completing a full budget as per the template provided. How much would your programme cost if you had to pay for all your resources?

PART TWO

Action!

6

TALENT SHOWS

Talent shows are televised competitions and encompass singing, dancing and any number of so-called variety, from acrobatics, magicians and comedians to performing animals. Talented dogs are particularly popular with the audience of *Britain's Got Talent* (*BGT*), with a dog act winning in 2012 and 2015. The genre provides a platform for mostly undiscovered amateur talent to perform in front of a live audience and holds the promise of being 'discovered'. Susan Boyle found fame after appearing on *BGT* in 2009, surprising audiences with her operatic vocals and catapulting her to world fame.

Talent shows have the capacity to reach huge family audiences. During the 1960s and 70s there were only three TV channels in the UK (BBC One, BBC Two and ITV) and talent shows played a big part in the TV schedules, pulling in millions of viewers in their prime-time Saturday evening slots, and continue to do so today. Saturday evening television is all about entertainment and talent shows are at the heart of the Saturday evening schedule. The UK public service TV provider, the BBC and its commercial rival ITV regularly go head-to-head, pitting their talent shows against one another with ITV's *The X Factor* competing with *Strictly Come Dancing* on the BBC. At a Royal Television Society event on 22 September 2015 Richard Holloway, Managing Director of Thames (part of FremantleMedia UK), whose hit shows include *BGT*, *The X Factor*, *Pop Idol*, *The Price is Right* and *The Muppet Show*, talked about how to make a successful format:

> You want to make a format as multifaceted as possible with great punters and celebrities. You want to have a great format where you are engaged in storytelling, game play, personality, winners, losers, and can affect the result of the show. That's why I love *BGT* and *The X Factor*. It works on all of those levels – right up until the end where the audience can decide who the winner is, and that's important.[4]

In this chapter we will look specifically at the large global talent show formats that attract millions of viewers around the world, such as *The Voice* and *Got Talent*, with interviews with top executives in China and Australia discussing the differences across international territories. Towards the end of this chapter you will find a real-world script of *BGT* to practise in the studio and to help you make your own talent show versions.

Brief History of the Talent Show

The contemporary talent show format was born out of variety shows and began life in music halls in the UK during the eighteenth and nineteenth centuries. It then progressed to theatre and then radio before becoming hugely popular on TV screens in the 1950s with *Opportunity Knocks*.

Opportunity Knocks started life as a radio talent show in 1949 and first aired on ITV in 1956, returning for short stints in the 1960s and 70s before being revived in the 1980s by the BBC – with Bob Monkhouse as the host and renamed *Bob Says Opportunity Knocks* – and finally in the 1990s with Les Dawson presenting. In the ITV version of *Opportunity Knocks* the viewing public decided the winner. This was long before the internet and mobile phones so the show relied on postal votes. The later BBC version was the first show to feature telephone voting in the UK and paved the way for increasing audience interactivity that is now the norm in today's talent formats, with big entertainment formats introducing their own apps to directly connect and communicate with their audience. In 2014 *The X Factor* introduced an app which over 2 million people downloaded.[5]

Talent shows have often been rested and then revived. The variety format *New Faces* (ITV, 1973–8) saw acts performing in front of a panel of judges who scored and commented on the performances, not always holding back in their harsh assessments. Sound familiar? The 1970s version didn't feature audience votes but the show was brought back in the 1980s, this time offering the studio audience the chance to vote for their favourite acts by pressing a button. The show was a huge ratings hit and although there was no prize money or record deal, like in today's versions, it helped launch the careers of Victoria Wood, Joe Pasquale and Lenny Henry.

Other notable global talent shows include the *Idol* franchise, created by Simon Fuller and broadcast as *Pop Idol* in the UK on ITV from 2001–2003. The format became *American Idol* in the US and aired on the Fox Network from 2001. It dominated the schedules but with falling ratings it was cancelled in 2016, after its fifteenth season. Both *Pop Idol* and *American Idol* featured Simon Cowell as a judge, with his rude remarks and 'pantomime villain' behaviour winning audiences on both sides of the Atlantic. In the UK Simon Cowell's similar talent format, *The X Factor*, with groups and no upper age, started in 2003. The show has had regular tweaks to on-screen and off-screen talent to keep the format interesting and gain young viewers who are crucial to supporting the show by downloading the music.

Key Ingredients

Over the years technological advances have meant that producers are able to capture every single moment with cameras into double figures. These big shows employ big teams to pull everything together. The post-production stage is fast and furious with stories changing and being re-edited right until the last minute as Richard Holloway, Executive Producer of *The X Factor*, *BGT* and *Pop Idol*, and producer of the 1980s version of *New Faces*, explains:

> Technologically, the differences are extraordinary. When we do the auditions for *BGT* and *The X Factor* we have somewhere in the region of 35 cameras rolling at any one time … We only had one location camera on the *New Faces* auditions, that was all we had! Now when you are editing, you put all the material into a server and then just pull it all out, hours and hours of material … You could say we have too many choices. We can construct one of these shows in eight days from nothing. But then with three days to go if you want to change things up you can. There are tons of stories in the server and you can juggle it up so it makes it harder because you have got those choices.[6]

It is an intense, high-pressure genre to work on and a strong team led by a good showrunner and producer is paramount to make a talent show. You are live every Saturday and Sunday night and being watched by an audience of millions. Traditionally you would do a rehearsal the night before, with a thorough block-through without cameras and then with cameras so that everyone knows what they are doing. It can be a huge buzz working on a live show like this, but it takes a lot of organising to get it right and a good team on-screen and off to pull it off.

Case Study: *Britain's Got Talent*
The format

BGT began life in 2007 on ITV. It is part of the *Got Talent* franchise created by Simon Cowell and produced by his production company (Syco) along with FremantleMedia. It is a huge international hit with local versions being made around the world. *America's Got Talent* (*AGT*) was the first of the franchise to be broadcast on NBC in 2006 and is into double-digit season runs. It has featured Heidi Klum and David Hasselhoff among the judges and reaches over 10 million viewers.

The format features a wide variety of acts of all ages performing to a panel of judges who decide if they will make it past the audition stage, held in front of live audiences, to the live televised performances where the viewers at home get to vote for their favourite acts. The judges hold all the power at the audition stage but are influenced by the live audience reaction – whether it's a standing ovation or booing – and can cut short an act's performance by

Image 5 *Britain's Got Talent* judges (Courtesy of FremantleMedia UK)

pressing their red buzzer, which lights up their corresponding 'X' on the stage. If the act receives three X's they have to stop performing. The acts need at least three 'yes' votes from the judges to move to the live shows. If a judge is particularly impressed they can use the golden buzzer to send an act straight to the live shows. In the UK, acts compete to perform in front of the Royal family at the Royal Variety Performance and for a cash prize of £250,000.

It was clearly influenced by earlier talent shows such as *New Faces* but differs from them by including viewers in the behind-the-scenes audition process, involving the audience in this process. The storytelling is also carefully crafted so that we get to know the back story of some of the contestants.

The casting is an important part of *BGT*. It is presented by ITV entertainment duo Ant and Dec, and Simon Cowell co-judges with David Walliams, Amanda Holden and Alesha Dixon. *The X Factor* makes regular changes to its panel but this is not the case with *BGT*, as Richard Holloway explains:

> I think the panel is amazing, hence we've stuck with it. It's a really starry strong cast and plus when we cast the acts really well it's a really engaging show so it could run for many years. It's our most profitable show in terms of selling around the world. We sell it to more territories than any other show.[7]

The contributors are also a vital part of this format. The characters are given shape and brought to life with emotional back stories to encourage the audience to engage with the show and, importantly, care enough to vote. These shows are a lot more than just about singing or performing; they sell a dream. The show is very much dependent on voting as this creates not just revenue but the jeopardy of whether a character will progress to the next round or be eliminated.

The production values are high, with state-of-the-art dazzling sets with plasma screens. The audience can be involved in a number of ways, via multiplatform opportunities – and importantly once past auditions the public get to vote and decide.

Behind the Scenes – The Big Interview with TV Executives Adrian Swift and Rebecca Yang

Adrian Swift, Head of Content, Production and Development, Nine Network (Australia) and former executive producer of *The Voice Australia*. Rebecca Yang is CEO of IPCN, distributor of *The Voice of China* and *China's Got Talent*.

How do you adapt an existing format for the international market and what are the global format differences across territories?

Adrian Swift:

I flew to LA to watch a recording of the first American *The Voice*, we had Cee Lo Green, Adam Levine, Christina Aguilera and Blake Shelton in the red chairs, and it is one of those formats that from the moment when you see it work, you go 'This is the most fantastic thing I have ever seen!' The core of the idea is by turning the chair, you see whether you want someone or you don't want someone, you approve of them or disapprove of them [and this] is the one bit of the format that is common all across the world and which we in Australia sought not to change at all. In the Australian version, to make it a little bit more impactful, we did what's known worldwide, in *The Voice*, as 'the long walk'. We followed the artist from behind the stage to the microphone and we used lots of shots looking at the backs of the chairs to give a sense of the artist's point of view and add a sense of the tension before they sang.

There is a mentor component to the show, so each of the coaches has a mentor. We decided that the mentor component was rather thrown away, so we put the mentors in the studio so that the coaches could refer to the mentors when they are performing, to give more of a local sense. And I guess the other thing that is fundamentally different in terms of how it was adapted for Australia is that we would strip all the episodes that we call the 'blind auditions'. So that rather than having one a week as they do on the BBC and sometimes two a week as they do in the States, we would put three on a week, Sunday, Monday, Tuesday to build momentum. Road blocking in this territory works extraordinarily well and for *The Voice*, which was the number one programme in series one and series two in the country, and the number two programme in the country in series three, that strategy of road blocking for the blind auditions worked really well.

Rebecca Yang:

For a singing show like *The Voice*, the format itself is very formulaic. The settings are exactly the same, the way the coaches interact and give them a lot of references, with the 'do I, don't I' hand above the buzzer. There is a lot of imitation but it is done very well. The choice of songs needs adapting but the biggest difference was to give the show a Chinese soul, so instead of just another singing competition, our ethos on *The Voice of China* is changing the Chinese pop music industry. All of a sudden you have a responsibility, every single person there is doing something good for their society. It's not just about individual vanity. You can become the next so-and-so but the show itself is full of positive energy. To be successful in prime-time shows in China you have to breathe in those educational or inspiring elements.

The other talent shows, such as *The X Factor*, haven't worked in China. *The Voice* cut through because firstly it had genuinely great singers on stage with the best singers performing in the country, no sob stories, none of those wannabes, it was a genuine music performance of the highest standard so people really liked that. And the base of people who like music and singing in China is humongous, karaoke is everywhere so this sort of thing has a huge mass appeal. Secondly it was the first time that the celebrities, you know, have been lowered to the standard where they have to communicate with the contestant as friends if not lower, because they are begging them to join their team. In China celebrities are treated as superior beings, like gods and goddesses and all of a sudden they are begging the normal ordinary person to join their team – 'please, please!' It was so fresh and the celebrities really endeared themselves to the audience and the audience felt that they were so down-to-earth and they were not sitting on a high horse so that fresh element worked very well.

How important is the role of celebrity in the international formats?

Adrian Swift:

Celebrity talent is really important in these shows. It gets people in the front door. In the Australian market, we spend disproportionately more money on celebrities than they do in the UK, so unlike on the BBC where celebrity salaries are capped by the charter, on the Nine Network in Australia they're not and we spend a disproportionately high amount of money on talent. Our coaches in the last series were Ricky Martin, Will.i.am, Kylie Minogue and Joel Madden from *Good Charlotte*, so lots of overseas talent. Relative to the UK, relative to Italy, or France or Spain or the US, I think we spend probably more on talent. I think it works for the show. I think the Australian territory is one of the most successful for *The Voice* in the world.

What are the mechanics of the talent show?

Adrian Swift:

These shows are built on an industrial scale. So for example the production methodology is not that dissimilar to other big stripped reality
shows and you've got to remember, in Australia the airing schedule is much more compressed than other markets because we do
three shows a week. The blind auditions, the battle rounds and the
showdowns are the first three rounds of the competition and are pre-
edited and then we have five live shows in this marketplace. We start
recording in January and the last one goes to air in the second or third
week of August. So that's quite a compressed timeframe. During the
blind auditions there are four or five edit suites going, we never linear
cut, we're always concurrently cutting and we tend to divide production into two silos – which is studio and studio live, and factual and
storytelling. So we have a storytelling exec working alongside a live
exec producer and the sort of supervising exec producer sitting on top
of both of them and then there's my role, as a networking EP basically
sitting on top of them and basically co-ordinating from the network
standpoint.

The importance of interactivity

Adrian Swift:

It's important but the reality is, it's subsidiary to the main event. If the
show isn't there, it doesn't drive interactivity. I think we know from
looking at things like Twitter statistics that online activity, even catchup streaming, shows that there isn't a genuine correlation between
interactive behaviour and true overnight audience ratings. A show
can be a huge hit on Twitter but not work on TV and you can have
a huge hit on TV and generate no interactivity. Do people engage
more with the show? I think that what we've found within commercial television, certainly in Australia, is that we can sell interactivity.
Interactivity is almost more important, not because it drives ratings
or anything like that, but because it's a very easy way to get some
fulfilment around very expensive advertising packages for the core
advertisers in the show.

So in a show like *The Voice* you typically have five sponsors who have
full integration with the show in some way or another and then a
really deep involvement interactively in what we do around the show.
Is it important for the audience to drive an audience? If the show is
great, it's wonderful; if the show is terrible it doesn't matter.

What is the future of the talent show?

Adrian Swift:

I think the talent show format is struggling at the moment, certainly
in this market. *The Voice* is and always has been bigger than *The X
Factor*. AGT has failed here twice, which to a certain extent has got
to do with the certain peculiarities of the local market. *The Voice* was

down (2014) about 12.5 per cent year on year and The *X Factor* has been down 25 per cent year on year in this market. So we do think the talent genre is struggling. Does that mean there's probably room for creative renewal and that we can do something new and interesting? Yes! Will talent shows always survive? In some form I think we'll probably end up in this market as a one talent show market and it will probably be *The Voice* that survives and then give it another three or four years and you'll probably get *AGT*, or a similar kind of thing, back in around the edges. But of the three big worldwide hit reality genres, talent, food and home renovations (certainly the three big ones in this market), the one that suddenly has the biggest trouble here is the talent show.

Rebecca Yang:

I think this sort of Saturday night weekend entertainment will always be welcome on television because it reaches the maximum audience and audiences appreciate this big entertainment show, so you will never really find the format dies so to speak, but will it carry that sort of glamour and wealth factor? That is difficult to say. China is a difficult market to predict. So it is very difficult to say this will stick, that will happen so from the audience point of view they constantly demand new things so on the one hand, there are lots of opportunities and on the other hand it is really hard to maintain the longevity of a particular brand compared to here in the UK where shows can last for ages like *EastEnders*, for example. In China you just have to be adaptable and agile enough to accommodate whatever challenges are thrown at you.

Richard Holloway:

Entertainment programmes have a lifespan. What one has to appreciate is that *The X Factor* ratings numbers have gone down year-on-year but viewing habits have changed enormously so you have to look at the consolidated viewing and numbers are growing. People don't necessarily want to watch TV at the point of transmission and you have to consider that. *BGT* is the most-watched programme this year by a long way. *BGT* as a format is a more engaging format, it's got more legs to run, it's multifaceted with a lightness of touch and humour.[8]

Summary

▸ The traditional talent show has been continually reinvented since the advent of television to revive it for new audiences.

▸ Casting big celebrity names is an important element to the talent show genre and helps it get commissioned and connect with the audience.

- For a talent show to stay on top it needs to maintain high standards and often needs tweaks to reinvigorate it and keep it feeling fresh.
- Interactivity plays an important role in the talent show format but having strong content comes first.
- Talent shows are a hugely lucrative market with the potential to dominate global viewing – get thinking up those new formats!

Insider Knowledge

Adrian Swift, Head of Content, Production and Development, Nine Network, shares his experience:

The top three ingredients for a successful entertainment show format are talent, talent and a genre someone cares about. It's really difficult to do it with areas outside of talent, food and renovation – these are the things that always work. Whenever we try something outside of that they do not work. The one big thing all of these shows share is character. They're always built around characters. All the ones that work have a great character to lock on to and then the drama plays out in whatever genre we've chosen. Does it matter if the chairs turn? It doesn't matter if the chairs turn. Does it matter if the renovation is great at the end? It doesn't matter if the renovation is great at the end. No, it doesn't matter as long as the characters who are doing it are characters that the audience can engage with.

Now Try This

1. Look at the script of *BGT* and make your own version.
2. Finding the right contestants is everything – what makes a good talent show contestant and how will you find one? You can't just include people from London, or people of only one gender or race for a national show, which is why auditions for talent shows are held all over the country to

ensure a range of voices. Make a list of casting possibilities and strategies to find them. Think about diversity, regional accents, ethnicity, gender and age.

3. How would you reinvent *BGT*? It's about finding a unique spin so that it feels fresh to the audience. How would it be if you had different types of judges? What about if the aim of the show was to be as bad as possible and not get buzzed through? Play with the idea and break the format rules and see if you can come up with something new.

Sample Script: *Britain's Got Talent*

BRITAIN'S GOT TALENT

(SEMI-FINAL TWO)

[X] MAIN SHOW

(PRE-REC)

PART ONE

[2] INTRO SHOW & JUDGES

ANT:

Hello and welcome to Britain's Got Talent.

(RESPONSE)

Tonight is the second instalment of a week that's bursting with incredible talent, and we've got nine more acts determined to win your votes and a place in Sunday night's final.

(WALK)

DEC:

And they're all chasing that prize of a lifetime – a spot at this year's Royal Variety Performance and £250,000.

So, let's get going and say hello to the awesome foursome …

it's the Britain's Got Talent judges.

[3] JUDGES' ENTRANCE

(THEY ENTER)

ANT:

David Walliams …

DEC:

Alesha Dixon …

ANT:

Amanda Holden …

DEC:

And Simon Cowell.

[4] BACK REF LAST NIGHT'S FINALISTS

ANT:

Last night your votes meant that Core Glan-athe-wee became the first act to reach this year's final.

And they'll be joined there by the judges' choice, Alesha's Golden Buzzer act Entity Allstars.

And, of course, tonight we'll fill two more places in Sunday's final.

[5] CHAT TO JUDGES

DEC:

Right, let's have a quick chat with the judges.

David,

have you recovered from last night's excitement yet?

Are you ready to do it all over again?

ANT:

Alesha,

who have you got your eye on from tonight's line-up?

DEC:

Amanda,

your Golden Buzzer act, Revelation Avenue perform tonight – have they got what it takes to win this semi-final?

ANT:

Simon,

this year, we've got the semi-finals and the final in one week – how much more pressure does that put on our acts?

[6/7] <u>LINK TO ACT 1 VT: GROOVE THING</u>

<u>ANT:</u>

Thank you judges.

Right then, let's get going with the second semi-final of the week.

<u>DEC:</u>

First up is a dance group with a dozen members, but only one boy.

All eleven girls describe themselves as hardworking, dedicated and committed, while the boy describes himself as…

<u>ANT:</u>

Lucky.

It's GROOVE THING.

(END PRE-REC)

(<u>VT: ACT 1 PROFILE</u>)

[8] INTRO ACT 1 PERFORMANCE

<u>ANT:</u>

Please welcome GROOVE THING.

[9] <u>ACT 1: GROOVE THING</u>

[10/11] JUDGES/RIGHT TO REPLY

DAVID
ALESHA
AMANDA
SIMON

[12] VOTING DETAILS/ SEND OFF

<u>DEC:</u>

To vote for GROOVE THING call
09020 44 24 01
from a landline.
From your mobile call
6 44 24 01.
Or vote via the App.
But not until the last act has finished performing.
One more time, GROOVE THING.

[13] APP REF/LINK TO BREAK ONE

ANT:

Remember, for the first time ever you can vote for free on the BGT App.

You'll receive five votes per voting window which can be allocated to the act or acts of your choice.

This means you can spread those five votes over more than one act or place them all on your favourite.

Download for free on your tablet or smart phone now.

DEC:

Right, we're taking a quick break, but still to come tonight, we've got dog dancing with Jules O'Dwyer and Matisse, plus Amanda's Golden Buzzer act, Revelation Avenue.

See you in a few minutes.

(END OF PART ONE)

PART TWO

[16] WELCOME BACK

ANT:

Welcome back to Britain's Got Talent, where all nine acts have got one shot at impressing the judges and most importantly, you at home.

[17/18] LINK TO ACT 2 VT: J O'D & MATISSE

DEC:

Next up tonight are Jules O'Dwyer and her dog Matisse.

As I am sure you all know, Matisse the French artist was known for his fluid and original style and his daring use of colour.

ANT:

While Matisse the dog is known for his fluid and daring use of lamp posts.

DEC:

It's JULES O'DWYER AND MATISSE.

(VT: ACT 2 PROFILE)

[19] INTRO ACT 2 PERFORMANCE

DEC:

And here they are, it's JULES O'DWYER AND MATISSE.

[20] ACT 2: JULES O'DWYER & MATISSE

[21/22] JUDGES/RIGHT TO REPLY

ALESHA
AMANDA
SIMON
DAVID

[23] VOTING DETAILS/ SEND OFF

ANT:

To send JULES AND MATISSE to Sunday's final call
09020 44 24 02
from a landline.
From your mobile call
6 44 24 02.
Or vote via the App.
But not until we've seen the last act.
One more time, JULES O'DWYER AND MATISSE.

[24] LINK TO BREAK TWO

DEC:

Right, time for a quick break but still to come tonight we've got jaw-dropping dance moves from Bonetics and Amanda's Golden Buzzer act, Revelation Avenue.

See you in a few minutes.

(END OF PART TWO)

PART THREE

[27] WELCOME BACK

DEC:

Welcome back to Britain's Got Talent where the race is on to win a place in the big final this Sunday night.

[28/29] LINK TO ACT 3 VT: BONETICS

ANT:

Next tonight is a dancer who can do unbelievable things with his body.

DEC:

His audition stunned all four judges and we can't wait to see what he's got in store for us tonight.

It's BONETICS.

(VT: ACT 3 PROFILE)

[30] INTRO ACT 3 PERFORMANCE

DEC:

Ladies and gentlemen, BONETICS.

[31] ACT 3: BONETICS

[32/33] JUDGES/RIGHT TO REPLY

AMANDA
SIMON
DAVID
ALESHA

[34] VOTING DETAILS/ SEND OFF

ANT:

To vote for BONETICS call
09020 44 24 03
from a landline.
From your mobile call
6 44 24 03.
Or vote via the App.
But remember, lines don't open till the end of the show.
One more time, BONETICS.

[35/36] LINK TO ACT 4 VT: REVELATION AVE

DEC:

Next up are a twelve piece choir from East London – at their audition, they hit all the right notes.

ANT:

And in return, Amanda hit her Golden Buzzer.

It's REVELATION AVENUE.

(VT: ACT 4 PROFILE)

[37] AMANDA INTROS ACT 4 PERFORMANCE

AMANDA:

Ladies and gentlemen, REVELATION AVENUE.

[38] ACT 4: REVELATION AVENUE

[39/40] JUDGES/RIGHT TO REPLY

AMANDA
SIMON
DAVID
ALESHA

[41] VOTING DETAILS/ SEND OFF

DEC:

If you want to see REVELATION AVENUE in Sunday's final, you need to vote for them, call
09020 44 24 04
from a landline.
From your mobile call
6 44 24 04.
Or vote via the App.
But remember, you can't vote til we've seen the last act.
One more time, REVELATION AVENUE.

[42] LINK TO BREAK THREE

ANT:

Time for a quick break now, but when we come back we've got sweet sweet music from the Honeybuns, plus there's magic and mystery from Michael Late.

See you in a few minutes.

(VT: COMP- ETITION)

(END OF PART THREE)

7

STUDIO DRAMAS: SOAPS AND SITCOMS

Studio dramas encompass soap operas, continuing drama and sitcoms (situation comedies).

Soaps are usually set in a specific locale; a village (*Emmerdale*), a cul-de-sac (*Neighbours*), or a square (*EastEnders*) with a range of characters that appeal to a popular mass audience. Sitcoms are typically set in one or two principal situations such as the hotel in *Fawlty Towers*, Agnes Brown's house in *Mrs Brown's Boys*, or the apartment and coffee shop in *Friends*. In both soaps and sitcoms the choice of location helps to set the tone of the show and provides a sense of its identity.

The TV studio has multiple benefits for these kinds of high-volume shows. It offers the production team complete control over the environment, with no interruptions or delays to the schedule caused by sound, light or the weather, and provides the director with the flexibility of cutting from exterior shots of houses and streets to interiors inside the studio.

The UK has a strong pedigree in soap operas, with many soaps running for decades. *Coronation Street* leads the pack as the longest-running series in the world, marking its sixtieth anniversary in 2015. The USA has a stronger reputation for creating global juggernaut sitcoms such as *Cheers* (1982–93), *Friends* (1994–2004), and *The Big Bang Theory* (2007–), with episodes in the hundreds! The UK has created some iconic sitcoms such as *Father Ted*, *Blackadder* and *Absolutely Fabulous*, but they tend to be much smaller in scale and budget, with usually fewer than ten episodes per series.

Channels are always on the lookout for the next monster hit but it can be a difficult genre to get right, particularly with fragmented audience viewing habits. Werner Walian, producer of *The Fresh*

Prince of Bel-Air and *The Middle* explains the commercial pressures, particularly in the USA where they are dependent on advertising revenue:

> When I did *Fresh Prince*, we were averaging 26–27 million viewers in season three. Today, a hit is 9 or 10 million viewers and it's all about, for us, at least, the advertisers – are they happy paying for the 30-second commercial? When you break down how many commercials are in the show and add up the money, is that going to pay for the show? There is a breaking point where the advertisers are going to say 'now we only have 5 million viewers, we can't pay you a $150,000 for a 30-second slot, it's going to be $75,000.' So you have got to do the maths, but the great thing is there are a bunch of markets, you have DVDs, you have streaming and international, so there are other ways to make money. It's a different business today, but it will keep going as long as the shows are making money.

Soaps dominate the UK ratings figures and as such are at the heart of the TV schedule. The main broadcasters each have channel-defining 30-minute-long soaps that are stripped across the early evening on weekdays. Unlike other genres, soaps are rarely scheduled against each other so that a soap fan can watch all of the serials back to back, starting with Australian soaps *Neighbours* (5.30pm) and *Home and Away* (6pm) on Channel 5, *Hollyoaks* (6.30pm) on Channel 4, *Emmerdale* (7pm) and *Coronation Street* (7.30pm) on ITV, and concluding their soap viewing with *EastEnders* (8pm) on BBC.

In this chapter you'll find out what the key differences are between soaps and sitcoms. We go behind the scenes of *Coronation Street*, frequently the number one most-watched programme in the UK according to the network BARB ratings,[9] and there's an exclusive interview with executive producer Kieran Roberts and an opportunity to practise your own studio drama using the real-world example at the end of the chapter.

Brief History of Studio Dramas: Soaps and Sitcoms

Soaps

Continuing dramas or 'soap operas', as they are more familiarly called, began in the USA in the 1930s and were born out of radio serial dramas. Soaps were aired in daytime slots and their name derives from soap manufacturers sponsoring the shows in order to reach their target female audience. 'Opera' is a reference to the melodramatic storylines.

The first British TV soap was *The Grove Family*, broadcast on the BBC from 1954–7, but it wasn't until *Coronation Street* began in 1960 that soaps became a huge fixture in the lives of millions of Britons. According to executive producer Kieran Roberts, the success of *Coronation Street* is down to the blueprint provided by its originator, Tony Warren, who wanted to bring a faithful vision of ordinary working-class people in the north of England to the small screen:

> We were given a blueprint for *Coronation Street* from the very first episode by Tony Warren and I think there's always a blueprint that you would find in *EastEnders*, in *Emmerdale* and in *Hollyoaks*, and if you travel further afield you'll see the same ingredients. The first thing is, it's got a very ordinary community setting, their lives are sometimes extraordinary but they are not the rich and famous or powerful, and this is not a drama about politicians or royalty or glamorous celebrity-type people. This is a drama about very ordinary people. The sense of community and the sense of family and the sense of people coming together and supporting each other through difficult times is absolutely the heart of it. I think that's something you'll see on every soap.

Soaps are generally shot a few months in advance and filmed weekly across the year. They follow a number of storylines concurrently and have open-ended narratives that follow the personal lives and relationships of a community of characters. In the UK soaps tend to be set in realistic locations, but in the USA the appeal of soaps such as *Dallas* (1978–91), *Dynasty* (1981–9) and *Falcon Crest* (1981–90) was the glamour of entering into a completely different world of the super-wealthy.

Channel 4 began in 1982 and its flagship soap *Brookside* (1982–2003) played a key role in defining the cutting-edge ethos of the channel. It was devised by *Grange Hill* creator Phil Redmond and was filmed on a purpose-built cul-de-sac in Liverpool, rather than on studio sets, to increase the show's sense of realism. It set out to push boundaries by covering gritty topics such as incest and domestic violence, and is renowned for showing TV's first pre-watershed lesbian kiss in 1994. Phil Redmond also conceived Channel 4's still-running youth-skewed soap *Hollyoaks* (1995–) following the lives of aspirational teenagers in Chester. The soap uses social media platforms to connect with its target demographic and in 2014 was the first soap to join up to SnapChat, the picture-sharing platform.

The BBC didn't have a successful flagship soap in its schedules until the arrival of *EastEnders* in 1985 and it quickly became a huge hit, reaching up to 30 million viewers. It is filmed in Elstree studios and follows a community of East End Londoners in fictional Walford. It doesn't shy away from difficult subjects such as homosexuality and prostitution, and continues to break ground today with its no-holds-barred coverage of taboo subjects and live specials.

EastEnders' first foray into live broadcasts marked its 25th anniversary in 2010. To mark its 30th anniversary it went bigger and better with a series of live elements around the 'who killed Lucy Beale' plot. It was a huge hit with over 9 million viewers tuning in and it trended on social media sites. *Coronation Street* has also marked its landmark anniversaries (40th, 50th and 60th) with special live shows. These live editions resonate beyond the usual demographic and become a talking point, with audiences engaged in looking out for technical glitches and any bloopers made by the actors.

Australian soaps *Neighbours* (first shown on the BBC in 1985 and moved to Channel 5 in 2008) and *Home and Away* (on ITV from 1988–2000 and moved to Channel 5 in 2001) are an important part of the serial drama landscape in the UK and shook up the TV schedules, introducing the idea of soaps being stripped across the week. The soaps were particularly popular with a young audience. *Neighbours* reached over 20 million viewers at its peak and launched the careers of megastars such as Kylie Minogue, Margot Robbie and Russell Crowe.

Neighbours is filmed predominantly in Nunawading Studios, in a Melbourne suburb. The studio is where the interiors and garden shots are filmed. The studio is a five-minute drive from 'Ramsay Street', where the exterior shots are filmed. This is a popular tourist destination, particularly for Brits, where the show has a loyal fan base. The cul-de-sac is a genuine residential area where actual families live and are paid for the inconvenience of the filming that takes place, and for the disruption of the weekly bus tours. To retain the illusion that this is the real *Neighbours*, the residents are instructed to stay indoors during the tours and keep their blinds down/curtains drawn so that they do not spoil the fantasy of the show. According to Jet Wilkinson, director of *Neighbours* and *Home and Away*, the appeal of *Neighbours* in the UK has a lot to do with sunshine and optimism:

> It is the place you want to be! There's rainy England or Ireland and then you see people running around in shorts and bikinis on a beautiful beach and you are going to want to keep watching and keep escaping to that place! It's a great escapist television show.

Melbourne is not, in fact, eternally sunny, as the producers would lead viewers to believe, and can even drop to temperatures below zero. The trick to make it always look like the sun is shining is clever lighting and tight shots so that viewers can't see any rain in the background! It's also rare to find someone on a soap wearing sunglasses as it's important to see emotion in a character's eyes.

A lot can happen in a studio drama production like *Neighbours* and characters can transform in record time. Take the character Toadie, played by Ryan Moloney; through the wonders of television he transformed from being a troublemaker to a lawyer in record time, while Dr Karl Kennedy (played by Alan Fletcher) can seemingly enter a room and bring his patients back to life! The audience suspends disbelief and enjoys the escapism of these programmes.

When dealing with hard-hitting issues, such as teenage pregnancy, death and murder, it does so in a non-threatening way without using graphic scenes and there is no actual gratuitous bloodshed. Instead in a shooting scene there is typically one shot, you hear it and then see someone fall to the ground. Despite all of this high drama *Neighbours* remains an upbeat and positive show. No one is sad for long and if the audience is in danger of feeling down, the upbeat theme tune brings back an air of positivity.

Reality is not a key theme in *Neighbours*, with umpteen shootings, fires and crashes taking place in its quiet middle-class neighbourhood, leading it to be dubbed by many as the most dangerous cul-de-sac in the world. This illustrates the extent to which these dramas have to ramp up the jeopardy of the storylines, as this becomes a talking point and can create a buzz well beyond the usual audience. Drama scriptwriter Sam Snape says:

Writers are one part of a very complex production machine. Being a team player is critical. Keeping to deadlines is essential. Also, writers have to work skilfully with storylines which have been worked up by others and write, with authenticity, characters they did not create. More, the characters and the world they inhabit are often 'national treasures' and writers have to make them stay so. It's a highly skilled (and well-remunerated!) task.

The future of soaps looks promising with high audience ratings and investment in revamped sets from the BBC, ITV, Channel 4 and Channel 5. It is a challenge to keep a long-running series, stripped across the week, evolving but the genre continues to look for new ways to engage the audience.

Sitcoms

Sitcoms are often the hardest format to crack. It is hard to make people laugh, but when you do it can be a ratings winner!

The first sitcom, *Pinwright's Progress*, was aired on the BBC in 1946 but the format didn't become successful until *Hancock's Half Hour*, broadcast live in front of an audience, moved from radio to BBC TV in 1956 and made a huge star of the eponymous Tony Hancock, as the curmudgeon at odds with the modern world.

Dad's Army (BBC, 1968–77) followed the lives of volunteers in the Home Guard and started a wave of shows that are often referred to as the golden era of British sitcom, with *Fawlty Towers* (BBC, 1975–9), starring John Cleese as a rude and incompetent hotelier, *The Good Life* (BBC, 1975–8), following the trials of a self-sufficient middle-aged couple and *Porridge* (BBC, 1974–7), featuring Ronnie Barker as a prison inmate, all receiving popular and critical acclaim. These shows were typically recorded in front of a studio audience and used multiple cameras, allowing every angle to be covered to tell the story.

In the UK in the 1990s and 2000s, traditional multi-camera studio sitcoms shot in front of an audience became increasingly unfashionable. *The Royle Family* (BBC, 1998–2000), *The Office* (BBC, 2001–2) and *Peep Show* (Channel 4, 2003–15) experimented with ways to reinvent the genre. They took it in a new direction, out of the studio and on to location, using documentary techniques to change the pace and style of these shows.

Single-camera shooting became ever more popular on both sides of the Atlantic, offering a more filmic look. Werner Walian, producer of the multi-camera studio sitcom *The Fresh Prince of Bel-Air* (NBC, 1990–6), starring Will Smith as a teenager from Philadelphia who goes to live with his wealthy relatives, and *The Middle* (ABC, 2009–), a single-camera sitcom that follows the lives of a middle-American family struggling to make ends meet in the recession, talks about the differences between these two different ways to shoot a sitcom:

> *The Fresh Prince of Bel-Air* was my first series and it had a great energy! The actors thrived off performing in front of a live audience. The audience was a huge part of that process, but it's a different kind of comedy. The actors are waiting to hear laughs and you are getting reactions off those laughs. Single-camera is more like doing a movie and the comedy sometimes is a little more subtle. You do get to play reactions and build laughs but it's a different kind of laugh, so the actor isn't waiting for the laugh to calm down before the other actor can take their lines. There is a different rhythm involved so creatively, single-camera can look like a movie, and multi-camera can be like a stage play.

The popular US sitcom, *The Big Bang Theory* (CBS, 2007–), which follows the lives of geeky scientist friends in California, is shot in a traditional way in a multi-camera studio and recent UK hits have also returned to filming in front of a live studio audience. *Miranda* (BBC, 2009–15), featuring Miranda Hart as the socially awkward lead character, is a homage to 1970s and 80s sitcoms such as *Hi-de-Hi* and *Dad's Army*, with the cast waving goodbye at the end of the show. It intertwines some location sequences and offers a fresh approach with direct-to-camera confessionals. Similarly *Mrs Brown's Boys* (BBC, 2011–), a cross-dressing sitcom, reveals the mechanics of a sitcom to the viewers, breaking the fourth wall by having characters speak directly to the audience, and including shots of the camera equipment, crew, and blunders made by the cast.

Sitcom trends come and go but the studio environment is enjoying a renaissance and looks set to continue to play an important part in the future of this ever-evolving genre.

Key Ingredients

Soaps and sitcoms are typically based in real-life worlds and situations that viewers can recognise, believe and relate to.

The production and costume design play an important part in creating an authentic world, whether it's a street, a café, a family home or a hospital. The mise-en-scène of the houses where characters live, clothes they wear, cars they drive and their hair and make-up are all carefully crafted. Sets often double up as lots of different locations. Advances in technology have made creating bigger and better worlds possible. In *Neighbours*, Lassiters hotel is actually a two-storey building that is made to look much bigger by computer-generated imagery (CGI).

Soaps and sitcoms often base characters on sterotypes; the ditzy hippy one (Phoebe from *Friends*), the lovable rogue (Derek 'Del Boy' Trotter from *Only Fools and Horses*), the hard man (Phil Mitchell from *EastEnders*) or the long-suffering one (Gail from *Coronation Street*). They rely on the audience being familiar with these sterotypes. In sitcoms, personality traits and catchphrases are woven into the series narrative for comic effect, for example Joey from *Friends* will raise a laugh when he says 'how you doin?''

The producers of popular long-running soaps and sitcoms need to keep the fan base in mind, and scripts have to stay loyal to the characters' 'type' and the history of the show as executive producer of *Coronation Street*, Kieran Roberts, explains:

> The key is to have one eye looking at the world around us and making sure that the programme is fresh and relevant to a contemporary audience, while the other eye has to keep looking back over those 55 years of history and all those stories and all those characters and making sure that we don't lose sight of our roots and where we've come from and who we are and we don't forget what is the essential DNA of the programme.

But what is the recipe for a successful hit studio drama? Experienced producer Werner Walian provides his opinion:

> Having produced now for 25 years, you see the successes and the non-successes. You see shows where the scripts were phenomenal but the casting just didn't come together or you have a great cast but the scripts weren't up there. If you look at the history of sitcoms and you look at the shows that are huge hits; *Cheers*, *Seinfeld*, *Friends*, *The Big Bang Theory*, you can go to every one of those actors for a laugh and joke, they're all great. Whereas the shows that you see on-air that are only doing okay, there is always a couple [of actors] in that batch that are a weak link. So you need those cast members and that

script to be there for a successful show but then you can have a great show, but put it on the air, and all of a sudden, back in the day when *American Idol* was a huge hit, if you are up against that show, it's very hard, so there is a lot of luck involved.

Scriptwriter Sam Snape, with TV credits on *All Creatures Great and Small*, *Soldier Soldier* and *Casualty*, sums up the differences and similarities between soaps and sitcoms:

> Both formats have the same characters week on week but the way they work is different. A soap is a continuing drama. You need to have watched the last episode in order to follow the current one. Critically a soap will try and spin out a great story as long as possible to hold its audience. Sitcoms are normally complete in themselves. One situation comically explored and resolved in one episode. In both, though, their core characters do not change. They keep working out the same dilemma or flaw over and over again in different plots.

Sitcoms typically follow the three-act structure with a clearly defined beginning, middle and end in each episode. Soaps generally use a tweaked form of the three-act structure with constantly revolving stories, so as one story concludes another takes over. Act one is the first five pages in a traditional 30-minute drama and sets up the exposition, the principal dilemma and a sub-plot. The meat of the story is act two, where the story takes on unexpected twists and turns to add humour and keep the audience enthralled. In the last five pages of the script, the final act, the narrative reaches a climax but stories are not always neatly resolved. Soaps and sitcoms rely on strong endings to entice viewers to return to watch the next episode or series. Soap opera director Jet Wilkinson has this advice for how to build jeopardy with a cliffhanger:

> Pacing is important when you are shooting a cliffhanger, and that will come from scripting as well as making sure there is pacing in the actor's performance, an urgency or drama or poignancy. You have got to make sure that you shape that episode, so it has a journey and builds to a crescendo at the end which keeps everybody hanging and wanting more. Sometimes you can overindulge on a performance and think that it is amazing and dramatic and it is actually sometimes slow and boring so you have got to make sure that you shape the performance so that it has longevity for the episode.

Case Study: *Coronation Street*

Coronation Street is produced by Granada Television for ITV and first hit our screens in December 1960. The first episode was recorded live in black and white, moving over to colour in 1969.

It is fondly referred to as 'Corrie' by its legions of fans and continues to dominate the TV ratings as the most-watched soap in the UK. It follows the lives of working-class people in Weatherfield, a fictional area of Manchester in the north of England where life revolves around the cobbled streets surrounding the Rovers Return public house. It started broadcasting two days a week and is now stripped across the week. *Coronation Street* used to be based in Manchester's Granada Studios but, in 2013, moved to new purpose-built studios in Salford with a bigger set to better assist the requirements of filming for high-definition television.

Image 6 *Coronation Street*, Rovers Return Inn (Courtesy of ITV Studios)

Behind the Scenes with Executive Producer Kieran Roberts

Kieran Roberts is Creative Director Drama, Manchester and has been the executive producer of *Coronation Street* since 2006 and prior to this was the producer from 2002–4.

What are the pressures of working on a prime-time drama like *Coronation Street*?

There are a number of pressures, maybe the first one and maybe the greatest one is working on something that really matters so much to so many people, I mean it is and has been for decades a national treasure, a national institution. It really is rather more than just a television programme. There are a lot of people out there who have followed the programme for many many years. Quite a few ... have followed it since episode one and so there is an enormous responsibility to do justice to all those viewers but also to the programme itself. It has such a long and rich tradition and we have to be very careful with it, so I kind of see my job as looking after it for a few years and my first responsibility is as and when I do hand it on, it's in at least as good a shape as when I took it on.

I think the other pressure of course is striving to make the programme as brilliant as possible while coping with the sheer volume that we work at. We make more than 260 to 270 episodes a year, which is so many more times the volume of any drama outside of this genre. It's a unique challenge making that many hours of television drama and trying to make it to the highest possible standards. That is a huge pressure when you're on that kind of massive production line, when every day you're trying to create art. So I think those are the two huge pressures.

What is the importance of talent?
For me it begins, as all great drama does, with the characters and the stories and obviously a brilliant writing team, but if you don't have brilliant actors bringing those characters to life on-screen, then we're in serious trouble. But we do have brilliant actors bringing it to life and of course there's something that happens on a really long-running show like this that you won't get on shorter-form drama, which is a dialogue between the actor and the writer so the writer will create a character and put that character down on the page, and then we'll find an actor to play that character, but as that character starts to come alive on-screen, the actor will put something into the performance which the writer will pick up on and then you'll see over a period of months and even years, you will see what the writer's picking up, what the actor's giving them and taking it further so you get this wonderful kind of tennis match and so the actors on the show are hugely important. I mean the actors are obviously the public face of the show, they're the household faces and names. Their talent does so much to bring our characters and our stories to life but their work also does feed back into the creative process in lots of subtle but very important ways.

But actually sometimes you think you want a big star to come in and hit the ground running and bring this character to life immediately. I think it's important that we have a mixture of approaches to casting the show.

What are the mechanics of the series?
From the beginning we have a story conference with the writers. We do that every three weeks and the writers sit round the table with the

producer and the director and the story editor and the assistant producer and the script editors and the researchers and they talk about the story and where we imagine this character going next in their life. Over a three-week period, those ideas are hammered into specific storylines and those ideas are fed back to the writers of their scripts and then those scripts go through usually about three drafts and then they go onto camera, so from story conference to script commission is three weeks. It takes about another six weeks to get that script ready to shoot and then we shoot. We are shooting an episode in just over two days and we do that 50 weeks a year. We always have at least two crews working; sometimes you look at the schedules and you see there are four or five crews working at the same time and you see they are sharing the actors amongst them. So the shoot is 12 or 13 days and after that it's just a few days in post-production, editing, sound mixing and then picture-grading the episodes and then they're ready for transmission. That whole process from discussing the stories to getting the episodes on-air is approximately four months. So that's very very fast, but we're only delivering the episodes typically about three weeks ahead of transmission, so in the end we work very close to our transmission deadline.

It's good because it keeps us all on our toes, it keeps it fresh; it also means that we're not wildly out in terms of the weather – when the nights are drawing in and people are starting to think about winter, we're a couple of months ahead of that but it's not like we're shooting in the middle of summer.

How large is the production team?
It's a huge team, I mean we have about 250 people working on a permanent basis and when we're doing extra shoots, when we're doing big events, when we're doing stunts or a live episode, that team will expand by maybe a couple of hundred people, so it's a really big business and we are shooting 50 weeks a year, so it's pretty much non-stop. We have a little break at Christmas, where everybody goes and has a little lie down!

What are the differences between US and UK soaps?
I am not going to pretend to be an expert on American soaps, but from what I know of them, they play in daytime, whereas ours in Britain play in absolutely the heart of the peaktime schedule, so our soaps have a very different importance in the television landscape. The other thing, I have to confess from a limited viewing of American soaps, is their soaps tend to be set in quite glamorous worlds with lots of very beautiful people and that's just something that we've never gone for, our world is much more real, much more gritty, much more down to earth and it's not that we don't have some beautiful

people on-screen, of course we do, but I think we have real people on-screen. I think there's something heightened, something glamorous about the world of American soap and I think that's the big difference.

What is the future of studio drama?
I don't have a crystal ball, but I would hope that the future for *Coronation Street*, and the future for all of soaps, because the health of the genre does affect the health of our programme, is bright and long. I think this show is in great shape at the moment and [MediaCity, Salford Quays] ITV spent tens of millions of pounds building this fantastic new site. We had been in the old one for 53 years when we moved out and here we are in this brand-new one. ITV did not spend all that money for a short-term kind of plan. ITV as a company would like this programme to carry on for decades, never mind years, to come and so would all of us and so it's going to outlive me, I very much hope and you know, long may it continue!

Summary

▸ In a long-running soap/sitcom it's important to stay faithful to the original stories and characters. Popular soaps and sitcoms have a loyal fan base who know the stories and characters inside out. You can evolve them, but make sure you stay true to type or your fans will let you know!

▸ If you are creating a brand-new soap/sitcom then think about the place, the setting first – then develop the key characters; the matriarch, the rogue, the villain, the busybody around the location. Then you need a great script and a great cast to bring your stories to life.

▸ Scheduling is important to dramas. Stories are planned three-to-four months in advance and delivered about three weeks ahead of transmission.

▸ American soaps tend to involve glamorous worlds – such as the lives of oil tycoons in *Dallas* and *Dynasty* – whereas UK soaps and sitcoms are grounded in the lives of ordinary working people.

▸ Audience ratings are important, especially for commercial channels. Despite competition caused by increasingly fragmented television viewing habits, time-shifting, and streaming networks such as Netflix, soaps consistently dominate the top audience ratings figures, particularly ITV's *Coronation Street* and *Emmerdale* and the BBC's *EastEnders*. Sitcoms have the capacity to reach huge global audiences and are in need of a new hit. Get your thinking caps on – this could be your opportunity to create the next *Friends*!

Insider Knowledge

Jet Wilkinson, who studied media at university and is now an established TV drama director of popular soaps such as *Neighbours* and *Home and Away* in Australia, gives her top studio directing tips on getting the best performances out of actors:

> I think the best way of getting good performances from actors is to encourage them to play and explore so you are always embracing their ideas but at the same time pushing them to try your ideas or challenging them to be better, but at the same time nurturing and encouraging and making sure that they feel safe in a place that they can step outside their comfort zone and try new things. I think that trust is the most important thing between a director and actor, where the actor feels like they can be exposed and have their heart and soul open and then you will get the best performance.

Now Try This

1. Practise making your own studio drama soap with the script for *Coronation Street* (see below).
2. Watch your favourite soap or sitcom – stop it five minutes before the end (the final scene) and write a gripping cliffhanger/punchline that keeps your audience wanting more.
3. Get creative – try writing a brand-new soap aimed at 16- to 34- year-olds (a rival to *Hollyoaks*). Where might it be interesting to set it? North/South? An estate, river boat,

pub, university? Try playing with opposites – think about characters like Dr House in *House*, the doctor who hates people but likes puzzles. Remember place, characters, then storylines – get creative and see if you can come up with the next big thing.

Sample Script: *Coronation Street*

FROM: END OF EPISODE 8659
INT NO.8 PLATTS'
14:55

PART 1

1. INT NO.8 PLATTS' (ST4)

DAY 3   15:01

STUDIO   Callum / David / Gail / Kylie / Sarah

KYLIE, DAVID, CALLUM, SARAH, AS ESTABLISHED. THE QUESTION HANGS IN THE AIR. KYLIE EYES DAVID, HER HEART IN HER MOUTH. HE STAYS FIXED ON CALLUM.

1 DAVID:

Not that it's any of your business, but yeah. We're giving it another go.

KYLIE CROSSES OVER TO DAVID, SLIPS HER HAND IN HIS. SHE'S CHOKED. (IF DAVID IS FEELING DUPLICITOUS, HE HIDES IT BRILLIANTLY).

8660–1

_____

8660–1

2 DAVID (CONT'D):
We're gonna raise our kids together. Both of them.

3 CALLUM:
And they all lived happily ever after. Until Mummy Bear needed another wrap.

8660–1

8660–2

4 KYLIE:

I'm done with all that.

5 CALLUM:

Yeah right.

6 KYLIE:

Kills you, doesn't it? Me getting
my act together? CALLUM SNORTS
DERISIVELY.

7 SARAH:

(TO DAVID) You're out of your mind,
taking her back.

8 KYLIE:

You don't even know me.

9 SARAH:

Cage dancer, drug addict, unfit mother.

8660–2

_____
_____

_____

8660–2

10 CALLUM:

Fair play to her – she keeps her nails nice.

11 DAVID:

Bore off. GAIL NOW OPENING
FRONT DOOR.

12 KYLIE:

Least I wasn't knocked up at twelve.

13 SARAH:

Least I've kept hold of my kid.
GAIL WALKS IN. SHE EYES KYLIE
COLDLY. CONTEMPTUOUSLY.

14 KYLIE:

Hello Gail.

15 GAIL:

'Hello Gail'? After everything
you've put us through? 'Hello Gail'?
CALLUM, GLEEFUL, DROPS DOWN
INTO CHAIR.

16 CALLUM:

(TO SARAH)
Sit down, babe. We're not missing this.
AS KYLIE BRACES HERSELF FOR
GAIL'S WRATH.

CUT TO: SCENE 2
INT NO.4 WEBSTERS' (ST2)
15:30
8660–3

_____
_____

_____
8660–3

FROM: SCENE 1
INT NO.8 PLATTS' (ST4)
15:01

2. INT NO.4 WEBSTERS' (ST2)

8660–4

DAY 3   15:30

STUDIO   Dev / Emily / Kevin / Kirk / Luke / Rita / Sally / Sean / Sophie / Tim / Tyrone / Ben[NS] / Mary[NS] / Norris[NS]

Ben's Foster Mum / Maddie's Friend 1 / Maddie's Friend 2

BEN, SUBDUED, SITS ON SOFA,
PLAYING GAME ON HIS TABLET. SOPHIE
NEXT TO HIM, PERCHED ON ARM OF
SOFA. SALLY, KEVIN, EMILY, RITA AND
DEV WATCH FROM THE KITCHEN.

1 EMILY:

Of course once today is over, the hard
part begins.

_____
8660–4

2 RITA:

All the day-to-day stuff, but no Maddie
to share it with.

3 DEV:

They were good together.

4 KEVIN:

Poor old Soph.

5 SALLY:

She's holding it all in. All of this
'Maddie wouldn't want us to be sad'
business.

PICK UP SEAN, KIRK, LUKE AND
TYRONE BY THE BUFFET.

6 KIRK:

I'll miss her hiding stuff. Gaffer tape,
scissors, my packed lunch…

7 LUKE:

My monkey wrench. TYRONE LAUGHS.

8 KIRK:

She made the day go quicker.

8660–5

_____

_____

8660–5

9 SEAN:

I read that every morning Buddhists say
to themselves 'I might die today.'

10 LUKE:

There's a cheery thought.

11 SEAN:

Thought I might give it a whirl. Live
each day as if it's my last. Treat everyone I speak to with respect. TYRONE
AND KIRK EXCHANGE LOOKS.

12 TYRONE:

I give him half an hour. KIRK'S
PHONE BEEPS.

13 KIRK:

I'm gonna have to get off. Beth's on one.

AS KIRK EXITS, PICK UP SALLY, WHO
NODS AT TIM – NOW. TIM TAKES
SAUSAGE ROLLS OVER TO SOPHIE
AND BEN. BEN TAKES TWO.

14 TIM:

Good lad. Sophie?

15 SOPHIE:

No ta.

8660–6

_____
_____

8660–6

SHE CLOCKS SALLY, RITA ET AL
LOOKING OVER.

16 SOPHIE (CONT'D):

(WEARILY) Thought my ears were
burning.

17 TIM:

Sal thinks you'll waste away.

18 SOPHIE:

She's on at me all the time to eat. Or
sleep. Or cry. She's desperate for me
to cry.

19 TIM:

So sling a sausage roll down your
neck – get her off your case.

20 SOPHIE:

Off YOUR case, you mean.

21 TIM:

You can read me like a book.

22 SOPHIE:

I'd say you're more of a pamphlet.

TIM HEADS BACK TO TABLE. SALLY'S
OVER LIKE A SHOT.

23 TIM:

She's doing alright.

8660–7

_____
_____

_____

8660–7

24 SALLY:

She's too brave for her own good.

FROM SALLY, WORRIED.

CUT TO: SCENE 3
INT NO.8 PLATTS' (ST4)
16:01

8

GAME AND QUIZ SHOWS

Studio game shows and quiz formats are a main staple of the television schedule. As well as the fun play-along factor, they can also sell a dream, the chance to win an amazing prize that could change a contestant's life forever. Quiz shows tend to be defined by answering a series of questions, like *The Chase* and *Who Wants to be a Millionaire?*. Often these have an element of multiple choice to give viewers the chance to play along and guess the answers so the whole family can get involved. Game shows typically have more physical challenges, like *Ninja Warriors* or *Total Wipeout*, and involve extreme obstacle courses. And of course there are all kinds of genre hybrids in between.

Game and quiz shows travel well to other territories with multiple versions of a successful format being made all over the world. Many formats, such as *Mr & Mrs*, *The Price is Right* and *Krypton Factor* have all come and gone, had a makeover, an interactive twist and found themselves back on our screens in prime-time viewing. The game/quiz show lends itself perfectly to the studio environment, often with several shows being recorded in one day. This makes for a more cost-effective production. Every channel broadcasts game and quiz shows, whether it is a family-friendly light entertainment show characterised by Saturday night or more high-brow intellectual game shows for BBC Two. You will notice, charting studio game shows through history, how the mood of the times and the politics of the moment influence the style of presenter and the tone of the show, whether it's the material wealth and prizes of the 80s, with formats like *The Price is Right*, through to more personal challenges and extreme nature of the noughties with shows like *Ninja Warriors*.

In this chapter we look at the global hit *The Chase* and go behind the scenes with the show's executive producer to see what it takes to come up with the winning formula for a game show.

Brief History of the Game and Quiz Show

In 1938 *Spelling Bee* began broadcasting live from the BBC and launched what was to become one of the most popular genres on television. The BBC, which is publicly funded, avoided big game show prizes in these early days, as it did not sit well with their remit. But the launch of ITV, the UK's first commercial station, changed that. The new network brought with it adverts and then prize funds. *Take Your Pick* was the first to offer cash prizes, then *Double Your Money* offered a top prize of £1,000. By 1957, the winning pot was worth over £5,000 – slightly different to the £1,000,000 prize funds of today! Game shows were hitting peak viewing figures. ITV broadcast quiz shows six nights a week with hits like *Criss Cross Quiz*, *Dotto*, and *Twenty One*, many of these formats originating from the US.

The next key format development was in the 1980s with the birth of the adventure game show with shows like *Dungeons and Dragons* (a fantasy role-playing game). Advances in technology meant bigger ideas were possible, such as *Treasure Hunt* (solving clues with the presenter jumping into helicopters to try and find the treasure). In sharp contrast to the bigger-budget adventure shows was the more classic quiz show *Countdown*, launched in 1982. This was Channel 4's first-ever-broadcast show and still remains popular today. The show has been given a twist for prime-time viewing with *8 out of 10 Cats does Countdown* – which merges a comedy show with the original quiz show format. Can you think of other shows you could merge to create an interesting spin on an old format?

Although money was still a massive draw in the 1980s, with successful shows like *The Price is Right*, it was also all about making the people the stars. Practical joke format *Game for a Laugh* reached huge audiences, then dating came under the spotlight in *Blind Date*. We also saw the launch of the classic light entertainment shows, making presenter Noel Edmonds the king of Saturday night. These were riskier live shows where no one quite knew what might happen next. Today, this slot is mastered and dominated by cheeky Geordies Ant and Dec, with shows such as *Ant and Dec's Saturday Night Takeaway* where a lucky audience member gets to win the ads, but the shows are mainly a vehicle for the two stars to entertain with a mixture of sketches, stunts and challenges. Game shows often depend on the personality of the host.

The 1990s saw much bigger and more extravagant studio shows such as *You Bet* (where a panel would bet on the outcome of stunts to win points). The bar for what contestants were prepared to do to be on-screen was raised year-on-year. There seemed no limit to what could be done. In stark contrast to these 'shiny floor shows' was the very straightforward comedy panel show format, *Have I Got News for You*, which saw five personalities sitting on a panel in a simple set. It was a genre trailblazer and many others followed the trend in wider topics such as sport and music.

In 1993, the regulators removed the prize limit that could be given away on game shows. As negative equity was rife throughout the UK, *Raise the Roof* sold escapism with a free £100,000 house. 1998 saw the start of ITV's *Who Wants to be a Millionaire?* This began a whole new breed of game show. *Who Wants to be a Millionaire?* was difficult for the BBC who, lacking the huge prize pots, were at a loss to compete with the success of the show. They were forced to find an alternative ratings-winner using jeopardy. They eventually found success with series like *Friends Like These* and *Weakest Link*. The format relied upon personal alliances rather than big prizes. These formats became hits on a global scale, proving that it was not always about the money – but it did demonstrate the power of the host to create the drama. Presenter Anne Robinson's catchphrases and steely persona was the making of *Weakest Link*, with *'you are the weakest link – goodbye'* (and for *Who Wants to be a Millionaire?*, *'is that your final answer?'*) becoming engrained in the public's psyche.

At the beginning of the noughties it seemed like game shows were losing their appeal. So, in 2005, when Endemol's *Deal or No Deal* arrived as the first new game show in years, it made big news. It had a £250,000 prize pot, which was unheard of for a daytime format. Together with *Ant and Dec's Gameshow Marathon* the genre was revitalised and subsequently many old favourites (*Bullseye, The Price is Right, Family Fortunes*) staged a comeback too.

Martin Scott, executive producer of *The Chase* and *Ninja Warrior UK*, and former producer for *Weakest Link* and *Who Wants to be a Millionaire?*, says:

> In a sense television is cyclical, you know there was a time before *Who Wants to be a Millionaire?* when nobody was putting game shows and quiz shows on. There was nothing and suddenly *Millionaire* changed

all that, and then it dipped a little. Now it seems to be bouncing back again. But I think *Ninja Warrior* has made a show comeback in that physical game show arena and I think there will be lot more physical game shows around on our screens. Physical game shows and quiz shows I think are going to be quite strong for a while and people like them. There isn't very much of quiz shows in prime-time during the week. There doesn't seem to be much appetite for that which surprises me. I think maybe that might change a little bit, but daytime (4pm, 5pm slot) seems to be the home of quiz at the moment. I think that will probably stay the same for quite a while.

Key Ingredients

As with all shows, the USP (unique selling point) needs to be clear. What makes your game show or quiz show different? Essentially all will have question or challenge rounds but what is the concept that hangs it together? What is the twist? So in *The Chase* they are trying to beat the world's best quiz brains; in *Million Pound Drop* they begin with a million pounds and fight to hold on to it through a series of multiple choice questions, painfully watching the cash fall away as they get the questions wrong. These format points then give the production designers something to work to as they develop the set and lighting plans to create the drama. When you look at early incarnations of the most successful quiz shows in the pilot stage, they look a lot different to the final product with dimmed lights, tension music and slick sets.

Martin Scott explains the importance of the set:

> With *The Chase*, very much it is about the intimidation of the chaser which is trying to catch you all the time – so the idea was to put them up high up above, so when you are standing at the bottom of the table, with a host there and the contestant there and you are having to look up at the chaser it makes it very intimidating. Then obviously the graphics are in the table so you can actually see as a contestant [that the] chaser is actually coming towards you if you don't get your questions right, so that becomes an intimidating moment as well. So the set was really key, a key part of that original design when we did it. It works really well.

Part of the success of these formats is the talent; often it becomes their show, with their name attached in the title. The presenter can really help build the tension. They ask questions like 'what would it mean to you to win this money?' to tease out the contestant's story. We want the audience at home to be rooting for them to win against the odds. They are also masters at coming up with catch-phrases that help make your show stick in the viewers' minds. Try and think up a new catchphrase for your studio show. The presenter can also be used to revive an old format for a new audience – think *Vernon Kay's All Star Family Fortunes* for example. The host's popularity can bring viewers and a new spin to an old show.

Having a good question-setter for quiz shows is also very important. Your show may need hundreds of questions or maybe just five. Questions need to be entertaining or challenging to fit the tone of your show. Questions with an unusual fact that can be discussed can add to the entertainment value of your show, leaving your audience saying 'crikey I didn't know that!'

It is not always easy to know if you have a winning format. Game and quiz shows need lots of testing at the development stage. It is so important to play the game – test it to see if it works and check if contestants understand the rules. Will viewers be able to connect with it? You need to look at it from every single format point and think if that happens and if this happens will this work? So you just have to keep running it and keep running it because there is always something that is going to trip you up, always that thing that could happen that you think 'I wasn't expecting that to happen.' You also need to work out what the probability is of the contestant winning the major prize. If you have a big prize at stake (like a million pounds), will you still be in business if someone wins on every show? This needs to be carefully mapped and considered.

Martin Scott believes playability is one of the key ingredients for a successful game show:

> Key ingredients … would be play-along-ability, which isn't even really a word, but … if you enjoy watching the show and every aspect of the show … do the key format points across the show make you want to play along? If it is a show where you can't play along, it needs to make you want to watch the next section of the show. So those are really the key elements, on *Who Wants to be a Millionaire?* which I was involved in, that took five years to develop and quite a lot of that development was all about what is engaging about it? How many questions are we putting in? Okay so it is for a million pounds, but is anybody ever going to win that? So you have always got to know [the] format, that you can actually win the money. It is possible,

rather than shows where you go in, [for] example *Million Pound Drop*, when you are starting with £1 million and you are reducing it, that is never as good as being able to achieve something much higher rather than starting with the money and then at the end of it you could end up walking away with nothing.

So think about your USP, the style of questions, the set, the presenter and the playability factor to create a successful game and quiz show.

Gameshow Case Study: *The Chase*

The Chase is a hit British television quiz show, broadcast on ITV and shown in countries around the world. By 2012, *The Chase* had become ITV's most popular teatime hit since *The Paul O'Grady Show* in 2005, and later achieved audiences in excess of 5 million. The production company make 190 shows a year and about 16–18 celebrity specials for peak-time viewing.

Image 7 *The Chase* (Courtesy of ITV Studios)

Hosted by Bradley Walsh, contestants must answer general knowledge questions and play their tactics right in order to get themselves into the Final Chase, where they could win a shared pot of thousands of pounds. Standing in their way is the chaser, one of Britain's finest quiz brains. The quiz genius chases contestants down the board in a general knowledge battle. If they get caught they are out of the game. As the shows says, *stay ahead of the Chaser and they share the pot; get caught and they lose the lot!*

Behind the Scenes with *The Chase*'s Executive Producer Martin Scott

Martin Scott is an extremely experienced game show executive producer with credits for *Surprise, Surprise, Blind Date, Weakest Link*, and *Who Wants to be a Millionaire?* to name some. We asked him about what it takes to run a high-profile game show, creating 190+ shows of compelling television a year.

How was *The Chase* developed?
The Chase was developed jointly by a development team and somebody called Chris Jepp. They wondered what would it be like if a big brain was chasing you. Would they catch you? And we thought that was quite an interesting thought. We went and developed it and it went to run-through stage. The idea had gone to the Head of Daytime at that point and she was looking at it and by chance Bradley Walsh was in for a meeting and she asked have you seen this? It was literally just on paper. And Bradley said yes, I like that! Why don't you come in for a run-through? Next week? And I can host it if you want! So he came in, he hosted it, he loved it, and that was it.

What are the pressures of working on a high-volume, high-profile show?
The pressures tend to be things like planning. Planning is so important. When you're making 190 shows, we shoot in blocks of four days a week, shoot three shows a day and each show has four contestants. So that means 190 shows that have contestants that you have to cast. We might have 130 questions per show, so for 190 shows that is an awful lot of questions that we have to write. So it is all about being really organised from the production team point of view, making sure you have got very good people, good question producers, casting producers and then surrounding yourself with a really strong technical team so when you get in the studio it runs like a machine. You can't afford to stop, so you just have to make sure that all the people are absolutely across everything.

What is the importance of talent in this genre?

It is very interesting actually, because there was a time on daytime when big talent wasn't really interested in it at all. And then I think gradually there are more and more recognised talent that want to do game shows, quiz shows, because they recognise the value of it and with Bradley Walsh (presenter of *The Chase*) he is on-screen effectively for 48 weeks of the year. So from a profile point of view it's actually very good for talent to be on-screen for that long and they actually recognise the value of it. Getting the big talent to do it is tricky because obviously they are not cheap, but when you are making the show with that sort of volume, it actually works out affordable.

How did you cast the chasers?

So with the chasers, what we do is look outside into the world of quizzing and we did a lot of research with people who win the ultimate quiz show challenges. There is a quizzing fraternity and they are out there all the time in the quizzing pubs and they have championships and everything else, so we started looking out in that area; quite a lot of people we looked at were very good quizzers but didn't have much personality, so then eventually after probably about a year, we found our first chaser and then a second one off the back of that and the referral, and we have just got a new chaser about to hit the air in September and it has taken us two years to find her and two years to train her.

Do you use a studio audience?

No. We have people there and we obviously encourage the crew to encourage them. And Brad obviously as a comedian and actor can very much play the drama one minute and then the comedy the next minute. I think that is what makes it slightly different from lots of other shows, because often you don't get that comedy. There are a lot of outtakes! It is really important that the set was able to allow Brad to roam as well between the chaser and the contestants and so it started in a very different way but it has gradually refined itself now, we have added more electronics and it looks a lot classier than when it started. We always wanted to make a daytime show that looked like a prime-time show and that was very much our visual style to start with and I think we managed to achieve that.

How many countries is *The Chase* in?

There is a lot of difference in the different countries, I think it is shown in 19, but more are being added all the time. Australia have just recorded their first season and we have got Andy Cross over to be one of their chasers. America is now on season five and Mark (The Beast) has always been the chaser in America. When America saw the show, they just wanted it, they just built the whole show around Mark, the beast, *can you beat the beast?* And in America the chaser is on-set the entire time, because they like having him there being intimidating for as long as possible, whereas we have him coming on and off. And pretty much, most countries stick to the format. It is something I learned with *Who Wants to be a Millionaire?* when we did it around the world, Paul Smith, who was the managing director of Celador, wanted it to have the same look everywhere, so whenever you turned on the TV in a hotel room, wherever in the world you were, you knew it was *Who Wants to be a Millionaire?*. I think that is what a lot of people try and do now. … I was involved as an executive producer on *Weakest Link* for quite a few years, and we put together a sequence of different shows from all around the world and some had tried to recreate Anne Robinson's dominatrix look, and then you just cut between [the] different faces [of] all of the presenters, doing exactly the same all around the world including Anne's famous wink!

Explain the mechanics of the show?
We have weekly meetings and we update ourselves on lots of different things. We have casting that happens throughout the entire year and we have a separate team go out and they are auditioning people around the country. People apply through a database and that application form is put on a huge database that we have and then the team go through the database and look at the applications and the videos that quite often people send in as well, we look through it all, and from that we go out to cast and we will contact people and then we audition them around the country and that continues pretty much all year round. So there are always meetings then about whether we have got enough people cast for the shows and whether we need to get out and audition more people. Geographical spread, male, female, diversity are all really important. At the same time there are meetings every week with the question producers and the question producers need to make sure that the questions that they write, the team of question writers that we have, are writing the right amount of questions that we need in the right areas, because we want a broad mix across contemporary, pop, history, geography, and we need to make sure they are accessible as well. So each question is written and it is graded in its level of difficulties, we [then] know whether it is a good question for contestants or not. We shoot for seven months, so next season we start recording in January and will finish recording in July, and will have made 190 [shows] by then so we are obviously then all about studio recordings. Then there is a massive post-production team that are editing 190 shows, because we are always up against that transmission schedule so we have to look at that all the time, so there are key producers in each of those areas overseen by a series producer who makes sure that [they have]

the broader view of all those other departments working underneath and their delivery dates and schedules.

How large is the whole team?
So we have got I would say, about 40 or 50 people when we are actually at our fullest, just to make sure that we can do everything and deliver our commitment of 190 shows.

What about interactivity and multiplatform?
We have got our own YouTube channel so you can see stuff that is shot behind the scenes or stuff that we have edited out or other little bits and pieces that we just tease our audience with. We have got Twitter all the time which runs every time we transmit, people are looking at Twitter. We have got the app obviously, that took about a year to develop, because we wanted with the app, format devices, we wanted to make sure that that was as close to the original show as possible, but that took quite a bit of time. We have board games, card games, quiz books, everything really, we are on Facebook as well. What is interesting is that the profile of our audience, the demographic, varies from 55+ who are great, who love the show and watch it every single day, and then we have a lot of younger people, then a lot of students, coming in the other end – so we have to appeal to quite a broad demographic and we find that interactivity is really important and they love it. They really love it, they send us comments about the show all the time, normally to tell us that we have got a question wrong!

What is the future for *The Chase*?
The future of *The Chase* is robust. It is ITV's top-rating show and there's nothing else in there that is coming in close to it so obviously we are very happy. So I think it can go on for years to come as long as Bradley Walsh wants to continue to do it, and people enjoy it.

Summary

▸ Studio game shows are a staple of the TV schedule. They take many different forms, from panel shows and adventure games to shiny floor shows with game show elements. How many can you identify?

▸ Old formats are often reinvented and repackaged for a new audience, so make sure you have some understanding of the history and context of the genre. Which show do you remember that you would love to see back on our screens? How could you develop this?

▸ Make sure you include play-along elements making use of multiple choice if you are trying to reach a mass audience.

▸ The set and talent can make even the simplest game come to life. Lighting can really help add drama. Work with your lighting director to see what you can develop.

▸ Essentially game shows all have common ingredients – there are questions or a challenge to win a prize. Know your USP for your own show. How can your title help to sum this up?

Insider Knowledge

Never underestimate how many questions you may need to use when you are at the piloting stage. You need to test your show with as many run-throughs as possible to iron out the detail so you really understand all the requirements of your show.

Now Try This

1. Practise your own version of *The Chase* with the script sample attached.
2. Like *Countdown*, a word-based quiz show merged with comedy panel show *8 out of 10 Cats*, try merging *The Chase* with another show – what do you come up with? Is it worth developing?
3. How would *The Chase* look if it was made for children's TV? What kind of characters would you have as the chaser? What would the prizes be? What kind of presenter would you have?

Sample Script: *The Chase*

		PART ONE	
		PRE RECORD CONTESTANT INTROS (SEQ 3A)	
1	CAM 3/ MS EACH CONTESTANT	NAME TEAM R-L SAY THEIR FIRST NAME, AGE, OCCUPATION & WHERE THEY ARE FROM	
2	ISO – 1/2/3/8 CAM 2 / OBLQ 4S CONTS – TITEN	**SEQ 1 – PRE TITLES** **HOST: (OOV)** These four people have never met before but by working as a team they have the chance to win thousands of pounds.	**CHASE PRE TITLES-** **1 SEC EDIT**
3	CAM 1 / MS HOST – TITEN CRASH OUT	**HOST: (IN VISION)** There's just one thing standing in their way – The Chaser.	
4	CAM 6 / DROP DOWN OS CHASER	**GESTURES TOWARDS CHASER IN SILHOUETTE**	
5	CAM 1 / MCU HOST	The Chase is on!	
		RECORDING PAUSE	
	EDIT / OPENING TITLES	**SEQ 2 – OPENING TITLES – GRAMS** (TITLES ADDED IN POST) GRAMS ONLY RT 0.08"	**TITLES TC10** **BED 3 EDIT**
6	CAM 6 / WS-SEE GFX ON BOARD/DEV TO 5S	**SEQ 3 – HOST INTROS CONTESTANTS** **HOST:** Hello and welcome to The Chase. Can a team of total strangers beat one of Britain's finest quiz brains and take home thousands of pounds? I hope so, let's meet them.	
		RECORDING PAUSE	
	ALREADY RECORDED	**SEQ 3A – PRE RECORDED CONTESTANT INTROS** SAY THEIR FIRST NAME, AGE, OCCUPATION AND WHERE THEY ARE FROM	

7	CAM 6 / WS HOST & BOARD **Q GFX ON DESK**	**SEQ 4 – HOST OVERVIEW OF RULES** **HOST:** And that's my team. Now one by one they'll try and bring as much money as they can down the table and into the team prize fund.	
		But hunting them down every step of the way is The Chaser. Anyone who gets caught loses their money and is out of the game.	
8	CAM 1 / MS HOST	Make it back safely though, and they go through to the Final Chase with the chance to win an equal share of that total prize fund.	
		And first to face The Chaser it's .... (NAME)	
9	CAM 3 / MCU CONTESTANT		
		RECORDING PAUSE **(CAMERA 2 REPOS TO UPSTAGE)**	
	ISO – 1/2/3/8	**SEQ 5 – CONTESTANT ONE AGAINST THE CLOCK** **(CONTESTANTS PLAY R – L)** **HOST:** And first to face The Chaser – it's	
10	CAM 6 / WS & DEV	.... (NAME) STING	**CHASE STING 1 REAL STR EDIT**
11	AS DIR / 1. MCU HOST 2. MCU CONT 3. TEAM 4. 5. OS 2S 6. WS 7. 8. 4S CONTS	 CONTESTANT BRIEF CHAT WITH HOST	**(SHORT STING V2)**
		HOST: This is the Cashbuilder round. You've got one minute to build up as much money as possible to take to the table.	
12	ON SCREEN / 60" + CASHBUILDER	Every correct answer is worth £1,000.	

13	CAM 6 / L/A WS – CRANE UP	And your time starts now.	
14	CAM 2 GFX COMPOSITE /		
15	CLOCK & CORRECT AS DIR / 1. MCU HOST 2. MCU CONT 3. TEAM 4. 5. OS 2S 6. WS & MOVE 7. 8. 4S CONTS	**60 SECONDS OF QUESTIONS FOR CONTESTANT**	EDIT CHASE CASHPOINT BED 1 MIN
16	CAM 2 / MS TO BCU CONT	**LAST 10 SECONDS**	
17	CAM 6 / H/A WS – FAST CRANE DOWN (LOSE GFX)	**LAST SECOND** **HOST RECAPS SCORE** **HOST CONGRATULATES OR COMMISERATES**	CHASE TIME UP FX C3
18	CAM 1 / MCU HOST	**HOST:** All you've got to do now is face The Chaser, but who will you be up against today?	
		RECORDING PAUSE **REPO CAMERA 2 LIGHTING CHECK REVERSE SHOT OF CONTESTANT**	
19	ISO: 1/8/3/5 LUMINA: CHASER SHOTS IN BOARD AS DIR – A / 1. MCU HOST 2. WS 3. MCU CONT 4. 5. 2S 6. WS 7. O/HEAD GFX COMPOSITE 8. 3S TEAM	**SEQ 6 – INTRODUCE THE CHASER HOST:** Will it be .... Or	
20	CAM 1 / MCU HOST	**BRIEF CHAT TO CONTESTANT RE CHASER HOST:** It's time to bring on The Chaser.	

	ISO: 1/4/3/8	**SEQ 7 – CHASER OFFER FOR CONTESTANT ONE**	
21	<u>CAM 6</u> / WS	STING	**CHASE ENTRANCE: CHASER STING C1**
22	<u>CAM 4</u> / MS CHASER – TITEN	CHASER ENTERS **HOST:** It's	
23	<u>CAM 3</u> / MS CONT REAX – TITEN		
24	<u>CAM 6</u> / WS		
25	<u>CAM 8</u> /		
26	TEAM REAX <u>CAM 3</u> / MS CONT – TITEN		
27	<u>CAM 6</u> / WS		
28	<u>CAM 4</u> /		
	CHASE ON SIT	MUSIC ENDS, CHASER SITS DOWN	
	(AS DIRECTED)	QUICK GENERIC EXCHANGE BETWEEN CHASER & CONTESTANT	

9

NEWS

TV news programmes play an important part in the TV landscape. All the terrestrial broadcasters in the UK include news in their schedules as well as running online news streams. The world of news is rapidly changing, with social media playing a part in breaking stories, but the BBC and ITV news bulletins continue to rate in the UK's top 100 network programmes.[10] Both channels schedule news bulletins at key times throughout the day (aligned with the times that people traditionally take a break from work, with breakfast, lunch and teatime) and a flagship evening programme. There are news channels running 24 hours a day. The first of these kinds of channels to hit the screens was CNN in 1980 and Sky, BBC and Al Jazeera are among the networks that provide a rolling news service.

News provides content for programmes across genres, from comedy panel shows like *Have I Got News for You* to topical talk formats like *Loose Women*, as well as informing current affairs programmes such as *Panorama* and political discussion on *Question Time*. News can be tailored for a specific audience as is the case with long-running children's programme *Newsround*, making news accessible to young people. The news genre does not just cover serious issues of the day but can include celebrity gossip and movie reviews, providing valuable content for breakfast and magazine shows.

Being abreast of the news, both in terms of popular culture and weighty world issues, will stand you in good stead for the media industry. Consuming local, national and international news stories, across platforms, demonstrates to future employers that you have a good general knowledge and are curious about the world around you. It also means that you will have a wider scope for spotting trends and formulating fresh ideas for programmes across genres.

In this chapter we will focus on daily live studio news bulletins with a case study of the flagship *Channel 4 News* programme. *Channel 4 News* has been on our screens since the inception of Channel 4 in 1982. Find out what it's like to run a live studio news room – where getting the facts right and meeting deadlines is crucial to the success of the show – and have a go at making your own news show using a real-world *Channel 4 News* running order to guide you.

Brief History of TV News

TV news was born out of radio news. The BBC began producing radio news bulletins in 1932, and played a key role in reporting news to the nation during World War II, building a strong reputation as a trusted news provider. TV broadcasts began in 1936, but were shut down during the war for fear of interception from the enemy, restarting in 1948. In its first incarnation TV news resembled cinema newsreels, with a series of filmed news stories.

It wasn't until after the coronation of Queen Elizabeth II, in 1953, that TV news was read by a presenter in a studio. TVs were still very much a luxury and the vast majority of the British population did not own a TV set, so had to crowd around TV sets in friends' or neighbours' houses to view this landmark occasion. With an estimated 20 million viewers tuning in, this was the first time a TV audience exceeded a radio audience and it started a surge in TV ownership. This news event showed that there was an appetite to see the news, not just listen to it.

In 1955 BBC newsreaders first appeared on-screen, reading a script. There was no autocue at the time and the sets were very basic so it's a far cry from the polished newscasters and state-of-the-art studios we see today.

The arrival of the ITV channel, in 1955, helped to freshen up and shape news bulletins. ITV recruited young, trained journalists, including Barbara Mandell, the first woman newsreader in the UK. Angela Rippon became the first female newsreader to regularly report the news on the BBC in 1976 and Trevor McDonald was the first black newscaster in 1973, reflecting greater diversity and cultural changes in the UK.

The way news is produced is directly related to changes in technology and the 1960s witnessed a lot of firsts. 1962 saw the first transatlantic transmission via satellite. The satellite revolution meant that the world became smaller, with news broadcasts being able to show images from around the world.

TV moved from black and white to a full-colour service on the BBC in the 1960s, helping to capture some of the most memorable moments of the twenty-first century such as the live pictures of men on the moon.

The dawn of global satellite links made 24-hour news possible. It transformed news production. It meant news could be broadcast live anywhere around the world, and brought into people's homes. Breaking news did not have to wait for a bulletin time slot in the schedule. The first UK round-the-clock TV news service was launched by Sky in 1989.

The internet has also had a huge impact on the way that we access news. News channels attract viewers to their online services with extra content, analysis and videos, and high-speed broadband means that news can be captured anywhere and distributed instantly. News providers need to have a strong web presence, as increasingly this is the way many of us consume news today. Job Rabkin, Commissioning Editor, Investigations for *Channel 4 News*, says:

> The audience on television is static, but the audience online is changing dramatically and more and more people are seeking out news online, news that they want to watch, when they want it, on their phones or on tablets. We have invested a huge amount in growing our online performance and we have a massive increase, month by month in the number of people watching our stuff on Facebook and YouTube. We also have the massive advantage online that the audience is across the world, not just in the UK. Obviously people watch different things online and they expect different things from the show, so it is a brave new world and it demands a slightly different approach to conventional TV.

News editors no longer wait to break the story on their news bulletins but post the story on their website first. Correspondents in the field need to be multi-skilled to write, shoot and edit packages and upload them to the web in record time to beat their competitors. Viewing figures indicate that young people are less likely to sit down to watch the news at a set time and there are now specific digital online news providers, such as Buzzfeed and VICE, that have expanded their news reporting to cater for a young demographic. The videos are not restricted in length and vary from 60-second reports to longer-length films over 30 minutes.

In 2013 when the BBC moved to its new premises at Broadcasting House with new state-of-the-art studios, they moved from using camera operators in the studio to instead using a robotic camera system controlled by computer software, allowing greater flexibility of shots with faster and smoother movement. This had not been easily possible in the past.

Younger audiences tend to seek out their news online and now everyone can be a part of the news. All you need is a phone or a tablet and you can create visuals and write stories. This is referred to as 'citizen journalism' and enables anyone, wherever they live in the world, to have a say and a voice and potentially reach a global audience via the internet. So it is not just the news editors who decide what makes the headlines, but this can also bring its problems as the information may be inaccurate, or difficult to prove, whereas on broadcast TV, there are huge teams of highly trained journalists to check facts on a breaking story.

Your audience relies on you to convey the facts. You will damage the reputation of the programme and reduce viewer trust if you broadcast misleading information, as well as coming under fire from Ofcom, the Office of Communications, a government-approved media industry watchdog. In the UK broadcasters are under scrutiny to offer a balanced, factually accurate and impartial view, particularly the BBC as it is funded by the licence fee and can't be seen to be taking one side over the other. Breakfast and daytime news producer, Lisa Armstrong, has this to say:

> If you see a story, and you think, wow! That's a great story! But you only see it in one source, in one newspaper, in one broadcast medium, it's not good enough. You have to have two sources, then it is all about check check check and check again! Check that it is correct. Check with the authorities. Check with the police. Check with the health department. Check with whoever that story originated from. Don't take it as gospel that whatever is written in a newspaper is correct. Often it's not.

News shows help to define a channel. Each channel has a strapline for its news output. ITN produces news for Channel 4, ITV and Channel 5, but they all cover stories in a different way and have individual visions and straplines that fit in with the overall channel identity. *ITV News* broadcasts news throughout the day at 1:30, 6:30 and 10pm. Its strapline is 'Getting Britain right 365 days a year.'

5 *News* began when the channel launched in 1997 and refreshed the way that news was presented, with a relaxed-looking news anchor standing, rather than sitting behind a desk, and this has since been adapted by other news programmes. It has also experimented with the news format by bringing on celebrities as guest editors, something more common on newspapers.

Key Ingredients

Good studio news programmes rely on accurate reporting, an authoritative presenter, strong stories and impactful images. Job Rabkin offers this insight:

> News defines a channel but there are still key elements that make up a good news programme. For a successful news programme on television I think it is about having strong pictures, I think the most important thing is the story; if it is a dull day and there is no news, the programme is generally not as interesting as when there is a big news day and a big news story and you throw everything at it. Pictures are incredibly important, the story is incredibly important and then the actual storytelling and how you weave that all together into a narrative that the viewer can follow … get all of those things together at the same time and it is a compelling watch and it is a great show. Not all of those things happen because you are doing it on such a tight deadline.

Images are an essential part of TV news programmes. It is important to capture your audience from the opening headlines with gripping visuals and your own take of the news of the day – whether that is exclusive interviews or first-hand eye-witness reporting. The bigger news channels have correspondents around the world so that they can deploy reporters quickly to be the first at the scene, and bring the audience unique access that rivals can't provide. Some news bulletins like to wrap up their news output with a funny or uplifting story, a format that became synonymous with '…And Finally' and Trevor McDonald on the *ITV News at Ten.*

An authoritative newscaster who is not just a mouth-piece, but can help write and shape the headlines, will help anchor the programme and gain viewer trust. These newscasters are identified with the channel brand such as Sir Trevor McDonald (ITV), Jon Snow (Channel 4), Fiona Bruce (BBC) and Dermot Murnaghan (Sky).

The studio environment is a crucial part of the delivery of the news. The set and branding add personality and are regularly revamped to stay modern and up to date. Technological advances in graphics and visual effects mean that news stories can be brought to life in the studio in a new way – making stories accessible to the audience. During political elections, for example, networks invest huge sums of money to win the ratings battle and use 3D technology to add a sense of excitement and drama.

Running orders are a vitally important part of producing a live TV news show. Typically the news editor decides which news stories of the day will make it into the final programme, and their order and duration, and this is all compiled into a running order (see the *Channel 4 News* example at the end of this chapter). The most important, headline-grabbing stories open the show. On a live show timings need to be carefully managed so as not to fall off air. Behind the scenes of the studio there are large teams of editors, producers and reporters busily sourcing breaking live news feeds, and the final running order will not be decided right up to and including during air time. This all makes working in a news room a very intense and deadline-driven job. Generally it is a 12-hour day with a shift pattern of working four days out of five in the newsroom. It's hard work but can be very rewarding.

Case Study: *Channel 4 News*

Channel 4 News is an award-winning hour-long flagship news programme, produced by ITN. It is broadcast at 7pm from Monday to Friday and at 6.30pm on the weekend, with a five-minute news summary at midday every weekday. It has been an integral part of Channel 4 since the channel's inception in 1982. It is presented by the respected national figure Jon Snow, along with co-presenters Krishnan Guru-Murthy, Cathy Newman, Jackie Long and Matt Frei.

The show is 55 minutes, so longer than the typical 30-minute news bulletins, and it seeks to offer the viewer in-depth analysis and coverage of the day's events. This is summed up in its strapline; 'engaging news and analysis for people who want to know 'Why?'' – it strives to be more challenging than its competitors and also mischievous. It includes longer-running films. Typically on news bulletins the news stories are 1-to-2 minutes long, but on *Channel 4 News* they can be up to 10 to 12 minutes to allow for the programme's original investigative reports.

Behind the Scenes with *Channel 4 News* Commissioning Editor, Investigations – Job Rabkin

Job started out as a BBC regional news trainee, working in Bristol and Manchester. He has worked as a producer on live political programmes for the BBC, and on the then *BBC Nine O'Clock News* and *BBC Six O'Clock News*. He joined *Channel 4 News* in 2003 as a producer and has worked in London and at their Washington Bureau in the USA.

Image 8 *Channel 4 News* studio (Courtesy of *Channel 4 News*)

What are the pressures of working on news programmes?
The main pressure is time. Obviously the show goes out nightly and the vast bulk of the content on the programme has to be generated on the day or just a few days before, so it is quite a high-pressured job. You will come in at 9:30 in the morning and often find that you are starting from a cold start with a story for which nothing has been done before or we did not know about. You have to do all the journalism, do all the filming, construct your pieces and get them on-air by 7 o'clock. So that is quite a demanding role.

How important are the presenters?
The presenters of news shows are absolutely essential to the character of the show. They are very closely associated with the show – Jon Snow has been presenting *Channel 4 News* for several decades. He is a national figure, people know what he is like and feel that they know him and trust him; similarly with our other presenters, they are all seasoned professionals who provide a lot of the character of the programme. When you watch *Channel 4 News* you expect to see them, you expect to see their interviews, and the way that they conduct themselves defines how the viewers actually see the programme to a large extent.

What are the differences between UK and US news?
In America, they have a completely different landscape. Someone once described it to me this way: they said that in America the TV news isn't particularly trusted and is kind of fluffy and not very in-depth, but the newspapers, the *New York Times*, the *Washington Post*, and the *Wall Street Journal* in particular are the kind of places where you go for the serious news. In the UK it is almost the opposite, lots of people don't trust what we read in the newspapers. They turn to the broadcast media to provide the real story, untarnished. I think one of the big differences between Britain and America is that the news programmes in Britain are regulated by Ofcom. We have a duty to be impartial, there are quite strict rules to make sure everybody's had a fair crack at the whip. There are rules about privacy and consent that are respected in a way that they don't have in America. I think that gives broadcast news in Britain a much higher credibility threshold. The American cable news networks, in particular the 24-hour networks, are dominated by opinion. So *Fox News* is full of lots of very right-wing, almost like columnists, venting their political opinions and similarly *MNSBC* is a lot more on the democratic side. Broadcast media in Britain is supposed to be impartial and that is a huge difference, so if we have somebody who is Conservative, we try to balance them out with someone who is Labour; there is always a need to balance things out in discussions which doesn't actually happen in America. I think the British broadcast media is also very much anchored by the BBC and the values that the BBC embodies and although I work in a

private sector, we are all affected by the standards that the BBC has, [and] we match or supersede those. That isn't the case in America.

What is unique about *Channel 4 News*?

There are several things about *Channel 4 News* that are quite unique. The first one is the format of the show. There are not really any other TV news programmes in Britain that are a news programme, a discussion programme and a home for longer films. The average length of a piece on the six o'clock news or the ten o'clock news is a minute-and-a-half to two minutes. The average length of just a basic news item for *Channel 4 News* is about three-and-a-half minutes and in most programmes we will have one or two films which are 10 to 12 minutes. So the thing about *Channel 4 News* is that it can deliver all of these things in one programme and it is an hour rather than half an hour so it really gives you an in-depth take on the day's events. The only other show that is similar is *Newsnight*, which has 4 x 15-minute slots and a lot more live discussion. It doesn't give you the day's news in the same way that *Channel 4 News* gives you the daily news. The other aspect of it is the fantastic journalistic ethos which is much bolder than the other mainstream news programmes. We will pick up stories that other people won't pick up. We will be quite cheeky often. [We] take on vested interests, do stories that are politically inconvenient. We touch stories that other people are a little frightened to go near and don't particularly invest in. Recently we really upped our input of investigative original journalism, digging out stuff that other programmes don't, so you get lots of original stories that you wouldn't hear about on other bulletins and there is always an emphasis on international news as well as domestic news. So it is considered to be a little bit more highbrow maybe than some of the other more mainstream news programmes.

How important is the studio environment?

The studio is absolutely essential and is the heart of the show. Apart from actually presenting the show from the studio, the studio is used constantly through the day. It is used for pre-recorded interviews, it is used for reporter pieces-to-camera for other interviews that go into packages and films and it is a very versatile space. Unlike a lot of other programmes we have retained human camera operators. We have quite a lot of cameras in the studio, two presenters and two screens, and the studio is really the front of *Channel 4 News* and that is what you see and so what the studio looks like, what the studio feels like is absolutely essential to our identity, who we are, what we are about.

What are the mechanics of *Channel 4 News*?

The programme editor, the day before they're editing the programme, looks at our diaries and what's been scheduled – whether we have special events that have been lined up, or guests that have been booked in advance. On the day of the programme we have a conference in the morning at 9:30 where we discuss what is going to be in the show that night and who is going to cover the individual stories, and there is a lively debate about how *Channel 4 News* should cover those stories. As the day progresses, stories often break and the situation changes. We have another conference after lunch at 2:15 where we go through how things have changed and what has happened. The running order is written and amended constantly throughout the day according to what is happening – it can change as late as five minutes to seven, one minute to seven; news can break at any time so we are constantly based around the idea of being flexible. About an hour before transmission our chief sub-writer will be working on all the leading stories and the scripts for the presenters to read; teams will be briefing the presenters on interviews, the presenters will be writing headlines of what is going to be in the show, we will have editors who are cutting all the sequences together, our graphics department will be working on the images that appear on the big screens behind the presenters, and the producers and reporters will be in edit suites cutting their stories for transmission. So it is a day that starts and then builds right through and gets up to a sort of very busy point about an hour to half an hour before the show actually goes out. It obviously ends at eight o'clock and then the senior management team will debrief the rest of the team about what worked and what didn't work and if something went wrong, work out why it went wrong and praise those who did particularly well on the day.

Who works on the team?

In the gallery we have a chief sub-writer, the programme editor, who is in charge of the programme and puts the programme together, the AP who is doing the timings, [and] the director, who is directing all the cameras and lining up lives and making sure the packages are done. We then have a vision mixer and an ancillary camera operator person who is dealing with some of the remote cameras and the lighting, and a sound engineer in a booth doing sound control.

In the studio itself we have the two presenters, a floor manager, and camera operators. We also have a chief sub-video who works on all the headlines and pictures for the show, then we have seven to eight reporters and producers on-shift at any one time on any day, and then we have our home news editor, foreign news editor, and forward-planning team, so it is quite a number.

What are the pressures of working in a newsroom?

We often have a number of people in the studio with the presenter and we have got to choreograph that. We have got to deal with make-up and sound and radio mics and keep it all going and you are turning people around constantly through the show, so Jon Snow will present an item, the item goes out, the floor manager brings in the guests, rigs them all up, gets them in position and the cameras are ready and that can be within quite a short window, and maybe a minute or two to get everybody in and out and the cameras in position and onto the next item, and the guests taken out without disrupting the show or appearing on-air or banging chairs and that sort of thing. So it is quite busy in there!

What's the future of TV news?

I think that the conventional news programmes on television will continue to decline in audience. I think the younger viewers are choosing to obtain news and current affairs in a slightly different way than watching television. I also think that demands of people's lives and people working longer and longer hours makes it difficult to sit down and watch an hour of news. I predict there will be a huge explosion in online [news] which is already happening. I think what we are seeing at the moment is that there is so much information out there compared to what there used to be ten years ago for example, that there is a premium on news programmes to invest in more original journalism; it is the original stories that allow you to be heard above the general noise. Everybody can see what the big story of the day is but it is those original stories, it is telling you stuff that you didn't know before that is really kind of breaking through and as the landscape becomes more and more crowded, you need to be original and dynamic, and this becomes more and more important. I think generally in the industry there is a tendency to maybe move towards sensationalist reporting of things. I think you've seen it in America with talk shows that they discovered that when they were politically opinionated and angry and screechy and all of that, they actually picked up viewers. The sad thing is people want that. People do want opinion and I think we'll be moving more and more towards that sort of thing and I think people will watch the outlets that fit in with their views and ignore the ones they don't particularly want to hear. That can be quite polarising in a society. It is a very different situation from when everybody sat down at the same time to watch the day's news programmes. I think we are moving away from that and moving towards a more fragmented landscape.

Summary

▶ Presenters are important on news – they set the tone of the show and help to build viewer trust. Newscasters can become trusted national figures.

▸ The world of TV news is rapidly changing and online news platforms are increasingly important, for younger viewers in particular. In the future there is likely to be a move away from everyone sitting around to watch the news at a set time in favour of watching news that interests them online.

▸ There are large teams operating behind the scenes with a programme editor in charge editorially and the studio director in charge of the visuals working closely with a team of five in the live studio gallery. The floor manager is in charge of everything that happens on the studio floor. News teams typically work a 12-hour shift pattern so that they can work long hours.

▸ The news TV studio is a high-pressured environment. Everything has to be carefully choreographed to run smoothly and it is important to be able to react quickly and calmly to the live news stories of the day.

▸ Images are important to bring TV news alive, and it is particularly important to use strong visual images when the presenter introduces the programme in order to capture an audience. The packages and graphics you use can set you apart from competitors covering the same stories.

Insider Knowledge

To build your audience you need to build their trust. Whoever the audience is you should always have integrity and get your facts right. It helps to start thinking like a journalist, as many people who work in this genre first trained in journalism. Know the right questions to ask to investigate a story and see if it holds up. These questions are referred to as the 5 Ws and 1 H: why, what, where, when, who and how. Deliver the news that your audience wants to hear, with accuracy, and you will build viewer trust and a strong reputation.

Now Try This

1. Practise your own version of *Channel 4 News* with the running order sample that follows. Go through the day's news and decide on what to include in your show. What is your lead story? – remember it needs to grab the viewer's attention.

2. Put yourself in the hot seat and see what it's like to be a newscaster. Write a one-minute script and practise using the studio autocue. If you practise in a team, get the producer to feed you a breaking news story that you have to report on with no rehearsal time! This will make you appreciate how difficult it is to be a news anchor, reporting the news live in a calm and professional manner.

3. Design a news studio set – think about the brand identity of your programme and the audience. Remember your set is the face of the programme. Will the newscaster sit down behind a desk or stand up and move around? Where will your guests sit? Draw up a set plan to show how you are going to do it.

Sample Running Order: *Channel 4 News*

No	Slug	Details	Pres	Prod	Appr	Legal	Print	Dur:	Forwardtime
	CHANNEL 4 NEWS								00:00:00
00	**TITLES-pretit**	ok	KGM		mjw		x	0:25	00:00:00
	TITLES								00:00:25
10	**TOP HEAD-leadin**	ok	KGM				x	0:22	00:00:25
20	**2ND HEADS-LEADIN**		CN*				x	0:29	00:00:47
	2ND HEADS-BOSLEY ulay				mjw				00:01:16
	2ND HEADS-SUGAR ulay				mjw			0:00	00:01:16

No	Slug	Details	Pres	Prod	Appr	Legal	Print	Dur:	Forwardtime
	2ND HEADS-SUPREMACIST upsot				mjw2			0:00	00:01:16
30	FEATURES-leadin		KGM				x	0:13	00:01:16
	FEATURE-CAMP upsot				mjw			0:00	00:01:29
40	AMBULANCE-leadin	ok	KGM	JR			x	0:30	00:01:29
	AMBULANCE-MCNAMARA vtr				mjw			4:14	00:01:59
50r	UNISON INT-leadin		KGM	MC*			xx	0:12	00:06:13
	UNISON INT-PREREC vtr				mjw			3:28	00:06:25
60	COMINGUP1-leadin		CN				x	0:09	00:09:53
	COMINGUP2-CARE				mjw			0:00	00:10:02
	COMINGUP-SOT				mjw			0:13	00:10:02
70	BOSLEY-leadin		CN*	MB			x	0:23	00:10:15
	BOSLEY-SONI live ex Bosley							0:30	00:10:38
	BOSLEY-SONI vtr				mjw			1:27	00:11:08
	BOSLEY-SONI live ex Bosley							0:30	00:12:35
80	ROADRAGE-leadin	ok	KGM	SW			x	0:27	00:13:05
	ROADRAGE-NZEREM vtr				mjw2		x	3:00	00:13:32
90	KNIVES-ulay		KGM	RL	mjw		x	0:23	00:16:32
100	PRISONS-ULAY		KGM	RL	mjw			0:51	00:16:55
	PRISONS-GOVE vtr				mjw			3:00	00:17:46
110	CARE-leadin		CN*	JO			x	0:24	00:20:46
	CARE-STING				mjw			0:00	00:21:10
	CARE-LONG vtr				Mjw2			3:48	00:21:10
120	SYRIA ULAY		KGM	MM*	mjw			0:25	00:24:58
130	FARRON-leadin		CN*	MM			x	0:18	00:25:23
	FARRON-prerec VTR				mjw			4:06	00:25:41

No	Slug	Details	Pres	Prod	Appr	Legal	Print	Dur:	Forwardtime
140	SUGAR-leadin		CN*	SC			x	0:27	00:29:47
	SUGAR-O'BRIEN vtr				mjw2			**2:39**	00:30:14
150	DEBATE-leadin FLEX		CN*				x[1]	0:13	00:32:53
	DEBATE-Aseem Malhotra x ST6							**5:15**	00:33:06
	DEBATE-Chetna Makan x ST6							0:00	00:38:21
160	SUPREMACIST-leadin		KGM	DF			x	0:38	00:38:21
	SUPREMACIST-LYNCH vtr				mjw			6:08	00:38:59
170	TENNESSEE TWO WAY-leadin		KGM	DF			x	0:17	00:45:07

10

FOOD SHOWS

A food programme is a television genre that usually shows recipes being cooked in a kitchen studio set. Food shows have always been on our screens with celebrity chefs defining the era, from Fanny Cradock's 1950s post-war housewife cooking, to the 'cool Britannia' style of the 1990s with Jamie Oliver as *The Naked Chef* who went on to inspire a nation of young cooks and a glut of new food formats. This saw a move away from the studio with chefs being filmed in their own homes, with makeshift studios on location. As is the cyclical nature of television we are now seeing a return to the studio with long-running shows like Shine's *MasterChef* and Cactus TV's *Saturday Kitchen Live*.

The studio environment is very important in this type of genre. The studio gives you control. Try filming in your own kitchen and you will notice how hard it is to get the shots you need. The use of the studio and the studio set allows you to set appliances and work areas forward-facing in order for the cameras to move around and cover the action easily. The studio lighting grid also gives more control over the types of shots used and gives the director freedom to use top shots, looking down on the food preparation. We like to see food looking beautiful and the lighting really aids this. Often the studio set is made to look like a chef's home. Many of the top celebrity chefs will actually go to the trouble of having a purpose-built 'television friendly' kitchen, with forward-facing units etc. put into their own home so it can be used as a studio set.

James Winter, executive editor of *Saturday Kitchen Live*, says:

> Studio television, it is all about control. It is about creating some level of consistency in production, so you don't have to deal with any outside factors. So it is never raining, the wind is never blowing, you can

generally contain all the cast and characters that you have got in a place where they come out and you can perform something. You are not always performing to a live audience, you may have an audience in there but you are really performing to the cameras. That is the beauty of having a studio, it allows you to be technically consistent and broadcast with some level of confidence.

Typically the show's celebrity chef prepares one or more dishes over the course of an episode, taking the viewing audience through the food's inspiration, preparation, and stages of cooking. Nigel Duthie is an editor who has worked on a raft of food programmes such as *Great British Menu*, *Nigella*, *Gordon Ramsay's The F-Word*, *Jamie Oliver*, *Barefoot Contessa*, *Angela Hartnett's My Kitchen*, *Food & Drink*, and *Ching-He Huang's Chinese Food in Minutes*:

> Recipes may take over an hour to prep, but you only [have] three-and[-a]-half minutes in some cases to show the whole recipe, [so] think carefully how you are going to represent each of these stages. Different shows have different styles with shortcuts to give an idea of what is happening, for example if there is a recipe that requires six eggs do you need to see each one going in? The style of Ramsay and Oliver is chop, dump and stir in seconds to keep the pace going – other shows are more literal. Know your show's style before you begin.

Food shows occupy every part of the television schedule and remain popular across all demographic groups. In this chapter we look at the long-running studio food show *Saturday Kitchen Live*, produced by Cactus for BBC One, which has been on our screens for more than a decade. What does it take to run a successful food show? And what are the added pressures of producing a live show where anything can happen and often does?

Brief History of Food Shows

In 1946 the first television cooking programme in the world was broadcast on the BBC. It was presented by Philip Harben and remained firmly on our screens over the next decade. Harben showed viewers simple cooking using available ingredients, such as steak and kidney pie and chips. He became the first of a long line of celebrity chefs that would grace our screens in the UK, each chef personifying the decade and mood of the time. Let's take a look at some of the celebrity chefs and shows that defined an era.

Fanny Cradock ruled in the kitchen from the 1950s to 60s. She was famed for wearing glamorous evening wear and inspiring housewives with some exotic cooking. In a post-war era her approach gave some much-needed fun and introduced the public to dishes from around the world. She is credited as the originator of the prawn cocktail! Next came Delia Smith (1970s to 2008). It was Delia's straightforward 'back to basics' approach that made her a household name. Her aim was to teach people how to cook and cover all the classic techniques. Such was her popularity that utensils or ingredients she recommended could sell out overnight, known as the 'Delia Effect'.

1982 saw BBC's *Food & Drink* hit our screens. It was the first British show on consumer items about eating and drinking, with reports from foodie locations across Britain with recipes. With a variety of different chefs such as Antony Worrall Thompson and Oz Clarke as wine taster, the series continued to run for 20 years. In 2013 *Food & Drink* returned to BBC Two revamped and ready to do business. This show is a good example of taking a successful format, updating it and introducing it to a new generation, a new audience.

Nigel Duthie reflects:

> On the series I worked on for *Food & Drink* the studio was actually the chef Antony Worrall Thompson's own home kitchen. This meant that the studio had to be brought to him. The show used professional film and sound crew with an excellent CV in shooting and lighting food. This saved a lot of time in post-production, syncing the cameras up, audio design and grading – as there was real communication between production and the crew.

The 1990s saw the launch of Nigella Lawson as *The Domestic Goddess*. She looked gorgeous, was not afraid to take shortcuts in cooking, and the food was carefully lit and shot and looked divine. It is worth watching the style of direction of this show – try and emulate the lighting and camera moves to achieve a similar look; you will see it takes time to achieve. The 1990s also saw the development of an array of popular food game shows. Combining the real jeopardy of all the things that could go wrong with a recipe with the drama of a competitive game show was a recipe for a ratings winner. *MasterChef* and *Ready Steady Cook* were both popular and helped launch the careers of many celebrity chefs from James Martin to Ainsley Harriott.

The end of the 1990s saw the rise of Jamie Oliver's career. Beginning as *The Naked Chef* on BBC his cool 'bish bash bosh' way of doing things, nipping off on his scooter to grab some last-minute ingredients, and his cool mates dropping by, made staying in and cooking for your friends the new going out! Nigel Duthie has worked on Jamie Oliver formats:

> Jamie Oliver's food shows changed the way recipes were edited. Directors were happy to jump cut, deliver pace, giving almost a grunge pop promo feel to it, which made food cool! It seemed suddenly overnight young people wanted to cook. The rise of the internet meant that if a viewer missed a part of the recipe or it was delivered too quick – they could be directed to the web to view the details online.

The noughties took the competitive studio food show a stage further by combining elements of 'reality TV' into the format. *Hell's Kitchen* launched in 2004 hosted by Gordon Ramsay, which featured new chefs battling it out to become the last chef standing. Ramsay, famed for his bad language and hot temper, really put contestants through the mill in a series of restaurant food challenges, as they fought to not be eliminated. Sticking with the competition–elimination angle, but in a much gentler tone, was new show *The Great British Bake Off*, where judges, cookery writer Mary Berry and professional baker Paul Hollywood, set out to find Britain's best amateur baker. The programme was moved to BBC One in its fifth series after it became the most popular show on BBC Two. Its increasing popularity is credited with reinvigorating interest in baking throughout the UK.

Key Ingredients

The most important things in your food show are the food – what are you cooking? – and the talent – who is cooking it? In a traditional food show that focuses on demonstrating to an audience how to cook a recipe, if you think about what you are cooking then the show can build around this. Often, thinking about seasonal ingredients or time of year will help focus your ideas. In the summer we want things like barbecue salads and strawberries, and in the winter pumpkin soups and roasts. You may also want a range of recipes, from starters through to desserts, to inspire your audience and build across the show.

So you may begin with a simple running order, the schedule of items in your show all carefully timed, that looks like this:

Item 1	Pre-title *On today's show we will be cooking...*	30 sec
Item 2	Titles	30 sec
Item 3	Chef PTC *welcome to the show* Recipe 1	4'30
Item 4	Actuality sequence/chat with guests	1'00
Item 5	Recipe 2	5'30

Think carefully about the running order as you do with all studio shows. Is your programme 30 minutes or an hour? How many recipes do you want to feature? How long will you give to each one? If you are allowing five minutes per recipe but to cook it in real-time takes an hour from start to finish, how will you cut this time down? It is not easy to do and requires advance preparation.

The home economist is an important link between production and the chef to road-test recipes. They will also prepare the food on the filming day at various stages so as to not delay filming while you wait two hours for a dish to cook. The chef will often have a preference as to whom they like to work with. Also consider where they will be preparing the food. If you are using the main kitchen to film in, is there a second kitchen that they can work in off-camera?

You will have spent time casting for your chef or cook to present your programme. They may be a triple-starred Michelin chef but can they work on-screen? Can they cope with the pressures of a studio environment, hot studio lights and time constraints? Will the audience be able to relate to them and be inspired?

James Winter explains the important ingredients for a successful food show:

> I think [for] any kind of show, the success depends on three things – I call them the 3 Cs. Cast, chemistry and content. In my world I always spend a lot of time getting to know a person that is about

to go on the show, so a chef may never have been on television before, he may never have cooked in front of anyone before, he may never have left his kitchen before, he may never have talked to people about what he does before, so I have to be absolutely certain that when that red light goes on they are going to be the person I believe that they think they can be, so that comes from experience, but also … some people I think get bigger when they walk on stage, some get smaller, some people stay the same. We will [be] looking for someone who will be a performer but we don't want them to become so much of a performer that you lose sight of what they are doing, because actually we love to watch people cook on Saturday, so casting is important. Chemistry obviously, you are going to put lots of personalities together so you want them to get on, but [they] need to be respectful and interested [in] what the other people are doing. It's generally not so much a problem with foodies, they are very generous people by their nature, their business is all about giving you a service, so they understand the process of giving, that is less of a problem. Obviously content is king, that is everything: what are we cooking, why we are cooking it today, how we are cooking it, what was the story for this recipe, what are we going to talk about with this recipe – all of that stuff is your bread and butter, that's your filling to your sandwich so they are my three things that I think about.

Think about the overall look that you are trying to achieve in your show – what is it? You may need to source props, tablecloths, plates, maybe flowers to dress around your finished dishes. Food is often aspirational and inspirational, but it can also be quick tips and food on the go. You need to match your style to your show's message. Are you trying to create a glossy *Nigella*-esque finish or a more 'cool Britannia' Jamie Oliver extravaganza with whip pans and handheld cameras? Are you planning to film in the studio or a makeshift one on location? Think carefully about how to handle a multi-camera shoot if out of the studio – you will need to sync cameras and probably do a couple of passes on a recipe.

Viewers really enjoy being able to go online to see the recipes in more detail. Think in advance about what additional content you will need for this activity. Recipe cards and ingredient lists that may be linked through to a supermarket, behind-the-scenes titbits and product testing may all be elements to include.

Case Study: *Saturday Kitchen Live*

Saturday Kitchen Live is a 90-minute studio food show, which first aired on TV screens in 2002 on BBC One. Fronted then by *MasterChef* co-host Gregg Wallace and later by Antony Worrall Thompson, *Saturday Kitchen Live* was packed with segments, from Michelin-starred chefs through to live cook-offs, as well as showing clips from the BBC archives of cooking legends like Keith Floyd and Rick Stein. The first series was a success, and *Saturday Kitchen Live* became a major BBC brand, replacing children's programmes that had been traditionally shown in this slot since the early 1970s. In 2006, independent production company Cactus took over production and *Saturday Kitchen Live* gained a more entertainment-based approach, with the focus moving away from simple suppers and snacks to more aspirational food with an increasing number of new chefs appearing. It is one of the UK's most popular food shows, with millions tuning in each week to watch chef host James Martin (2002–2016), cooking up a storm. The series runs for around 47 weeks of the year and is a staple of the Saturday Morning Schedule.

Behind the Scenes with Executive Editor James Winter

James Winter is a BAFTA-winning television producer and food writer. He is the executive editor of *Saturday Kitchen Live*.

What are the pressures of working on a weekly live show?

In terms of challenges, they are always the same – make 90 minutes of fresh, innovative, interesting programming. As producer you are really the only [one] that cares so deeply about your show, you are the one [that] is going to bring it to life, you are the heart that makes it beat, so if you still find it interesting, you will be pretty much certain that there will be a few people out there who will too. There is always a great phrase in television, which is 'if it's fun to make it's fun to watch'. *Saturday Kitchen Live* broadcasts at 10am. We try and be good company first of all. We have got to be respectful first of all, we are in someone's own home, they are expecting a certain amount of respect, some decorum, behavioural standard from the BBC, so that is what we have to stick to, but within that we also have to make them laugh and entertain them and inform them and keep them interested for as long as we can. Generally over the 89 minutes, viewing figures vary, but on average we get somewhere between 1.5 and 2 million viewers on Saturday. I think some people watch for half an hour and then disappear [and] another person sits down at 10:30 after having just got out of bed, so our reach is probably twice as many as that.

What is the importance of talent?
Talent in terms of being a celebrity and being famous is what gives you the star quality that makes television different from every other thing. We are all drawn to bright and shiny things, we are all mag-pies and like to watch shiny pretty people doing things; we can't help it, we are human beings and are drawn to that kind of thing. So you need someone who is more bright and shiny and fascinating and interesting than you are. There are lots of phrases that people repeat over and over again, 'talent is king' [for example]. In a way it is, if you see a name attached to a programme, you are already start-ing to form an opinion about what the programme might be like, whether you might like it, whether you don't like it, so if you pick the right talent as it were, to present, it will be a part of the front end of your programme; they already bring an audience with them. On BBC One we like to appeal to most people, and a broad spectrum. One presenter has to appeal to as many people as [they] can, but also they have to be an expert in the field.

Is there much difference in food formats in other territories?
Certainly when we are making formats that we get this side of the Atlantic [they] tend to be more entertainment-driven, more format-ted, they tend to be like *Cake Boss, Man v. Food*, they seem to be full of dramatic conflict and they tend to be less focused on recipes and ingredients.

What are the mechanics of making a weekly show?
Because we are a small production team of four, we are less regi-mented. Normally it would start with a weekly meeting with myself, the producer, the researcher and production manager. The discus-sion is always *who are the guests going to be?* Generally the weekly process will start with that along with *what are we going to cook?* Usually much of this is planned a few weeks in advance. Our first job is sorting out the logistics for the wine feature which we film every Wednesday before transmission. This is the only bit of original outside filming that we do on the programme. Again it is a very small team, a producer and a cameraman and a wine expert will go off for the day to shoot the film. I will then start the process of writing the script.

We have use of the BBC-owned archive to re-cut recipes from. So I will watch all of that through and then start writing the script. Then we will focus on getting our celebrity content ready. Obviously our show dynamic is driven by the 'food heaven and hell' theme, so we need to know what celebrities' likes and dislikes are as early as we can because then I can talk to the chef host and our team of home economists about what we are going to cook for them. The chef's dishes are the last part of the jigsaw.

I am very much a believer that people love to cook a dish they are passionate about, otherwise it will come across as just not interesting. So then really we are just trying to get a nice balance of different recipes with different ingredients and different cooking techniques across the 90 minutes. We get that done by about Wednesday and then we literally start the process of testing, testing, testing! On Friday we cook everything as a team and then on Saturday we get together very early at 6am and we do every word and every recipe, literally the whole show and then you have a quick cup of tea, check everything again, clean everything up and do it again live.

What is the future of *Saturday Kitchen Live* and the food genre?
Saturday Kitchen Live will probably go on for a long time. We are currently commissioned to produce shows until the end of next year. Then after that there will be a series of meetings and then probably some kind of tender process to see whether you get to keep making the show for the BBC. Certainly figures-wise, it still wins the slot and is still incredibly popular. People still seem to react to it and interact with it and enjoy it so I can't see the show itself changing in any great shape or fashion for a while.

Obviously there will never be a shortage of celebrity chefs, everyone is looking for the next Jamie Oliver. Everyone has been searching for a female Jamie Oliver. Everyone is looking for someone that can connect in the way that Jamie did, that not only changed the way we cooked, but changed our attitude towards food.

Summary

▸ Food shows need a lot of prep time and a good home economist who is organised with extra versions of the same meal cooked at different stages so as not to delay filming waiting for things to cook.
▸ Make the food look beautiful. It needs to look good and make viewers' mouths water.
▸ Be careful about editing recipes down. You can't cut out vital steps. Carefully time with your home economist just how much time each stage will take so you can find ways

around it if needs be. Will you show all six eggs being cracked into the bowl, or have them ready done?

▸ Talent is important. What is the USP of the chef you are using? Think of how you can sum up their style in a line. Is this food luxury or family meals on a budget? Your presenter and show's values all need to line up.

▸ The set is important – you may need extra ovens to help speed up multiple dishes. Where will the home economist work? – they will need a prep kitchen too.

Insider Knowledge

If you are new to directing food programmes it is really useful to sit in an edit suite and experience how difficult recipes are to cut down. You can't just miss stages out or the viewers will not know how to cook the recipe successfully. Continuity is also very challenging, as is thinking about what you are going to do while you are waiting for things to cook. What is your show's style? Will you have actuality sequences, will you use jump cuts, recipe summaries etc.? Maybe you can come up with something unique that hasn't been done before.

Now Try This

1. Practise your own version of *Saturday Kitchen Live* with the script sample attached. Improvise making cold dishes for practice purposes if you do not have access to ovens.

2. At home, as you may not have a kitchen in the studio, try filming a recipe on a single camera or your mobile phone device. See how long it takes and just what the editing challenges are. On the first pass see how long it would take normally if you were to crack every egg, keep going to the fridge, wait for the onions to heat through etc. On the second pass find time-saving devices. What will you do while the onions are heating through? Maybe start making

the sauce or film an actuality sequence with the chef to help show the passing of time?

3. In the studio, borrow food from your canteen if needs be, try lighting a static food shot of a finished dish, often referred to as the 'pack shot'. Think about dressing the set around it, light it and put it to music to create a 30-second piece. Screen your finished piece to the class and see whose food made your mouth water!

Sample Script: *Saturday Kitchen Live*

8 November
TX: 11.26

	Item 1 – PRE-TITLE
	((James))
	CAM 1
	Good Morning!
	No you're not dreaming we **are** on early but we're raring to go so let's get cooking!
	This is Saturday Kitchen live!
VT: MAIN SK TITLES DUR: 20"	**RUN VT**
	DUR: 00.20"
	Item 2 – CHEF'S INTRO & MENU
	((James))
	CAM 5
	Welcome to the show!
GRAMS: SK BED	**CAM 2**
	With me in the studio are two brilliant but bleary-eyed chefs.
	First, the man behind the Michelin-starred Indian restaurant, Benares.
	It's Atul Kochhar.
	Next to him is one of the world's greatest and most innovative chefs.
	His restaurant, Osteria Francescana is in the beautiful city of Modena and holds 3 coveted Michelin stars.

	It's Massimo Bottura.
	Good morning to you both.
	ADLIB GOOD MORNING
C/A ATUL KOCHHAR	((James))
	So Atul what are you making?
	KORI KEMPU
	((James))
	And Massimo, your food is known for being a little bit different so what's on the menu from you?
	ADLIB HELLO
	OOPS I DROPPED THE LEMON TART!
	(DECONSTRUCTED LEMON TART)
	((James))
C/A MASSIMO BOTTURA	So two very different recipes to look forward to and we've got our line-up of fantastic foodie films from the BBC's archive as well.
	Today, we've got Rick Stein, the Two Greedy Italians, and we begin the final stages of the Great British Menu.
	((James))
	Now, as I'm sure you know it's
VT: PACK SHOT 1 – KORI KEMPU	Children In Need's big night this Friday and our special guest has been at the forefront of the appeal for a staggering 35 years!
	Welcome to Saturday Kitchen,
	Sir Terry Wogan.
	ADLIB CHAT
	((James))
	What kind of food do you cook at home?
	ADLIB CHAT
	((James))
VT: PACK SHOT 2 – OOPS I DROPPED THE LEMON TART! (DECONSTRUCTED LEMON TART)	Now, of course, at the end of **TODAY'S** programme I'll cook either food heaven or food hell for Terry.
	TO TERRY
	It's up to the guests in the studio and a few of our viewers to decide which one you get. So, what would your idea of food heaven be?
	DUCK
	And what about food hell?
	SQUASHES
	((James))
	So it's either duck or squash. For food heaven, I'm looking to the classics for my inspiration.

	((James VO))
	I'd roast the duck and take off the breasts then serve them with some purple sprouting broccoli and a few duck fat potatoes. It's finished with a classic red wine sauce.
FADE GRAMS SLOWLY	**((James))**
	Or Terry could be having his food hell, squash.
	((James VO))
	The squash are pickled with baby turnips then served in a salad along with slices of rare lamb fillet, mizuna, mint and cashew nuts. It's then tossed in a spicy palm sugar dressing.
C/A TERRY WOGAN	**((James))**
	You'll have to wait until the end of the show to find out which one he gets.
ASTON – TERRY WOGAN	**TO CAM**
	If **YOU'D** like the chance to ask a question to any of our chefs today then you can by calling on xxxx:
	A few of you will be able to put a question to us, live, a little later on.
	And if I do get to speak to you I'll also be asking if you want Terry to face either food heaven or food hell.
VT: FOOD HEAVEN – ROAST DUCK WITH RED WINE SAUCE	
VT: FOOD HELL – PICKLED SQUASH WITH SPICY LAMB SALAD	
C/A CHEFS	
GFX	

11

CHILDREN'S TV

Children's TV is unique, covering every genre of programming from game shows, news and documentaries to drama, providing kids with a mini version of the adult TV schedule. Children are not a homogenous, one-size-fits-all group so it is important to know the age group your programme is for. It is about understanding your audience, as executive producer Maddy Darrall, who has an expansive career in children's TV, from working on the world's first children's news show *Newsround* (BBC, 1972–), to executive producing Cbeebies' first live-action drama *Topsy and Tim* (2013–) and the revamped *Teletubbies* (2015–), points out:

> The children's audience should be very segmented, what is right for a zero to three-year-old is different to what is right for a two to four-year-old and different to what is right for a three to five-year-old and so on and so forth. You have got to really know your audience. I can see *Teletubbies* appealing to six and seven-year-olds but certainly in the UK, a six-month-old might watch because it is visually engaging and it is not dialogue-heavy, and it is funny and silly... You've got to be able to naturally and instinctively breathe and feel your audience and have a vision in your head of who you are making this for.

In this chapter we will look specifically at studio children's TV programmes and give a brief overview of the history of children's studio TV production from the 1940s to the present. We feature a case study of *Teletubbies*, one of the most successful international children's brands of all time, having been broadcast in more than 120 countries in 45 different languages. At the end of the chapter you will find a script of the new series of *Teletubbies* to practise in the studio and make your own versions.

Brief History of Children's TV

Children's TV began life in the UK on the BBC in 1946, after the end of World War II, with just one 25-minute children's programme a week in the schedule, *For the Children*, not an inspiring title by today's standards but it certainly did what it set out to do! The programme featured songs, stories and a dancing string-puppet named Muffin the Mule and was presented by Annette Mills, who like other presenters at the time, was middle-aged and spoke the Queen's English. There were a distinct lack of regional accents on television. TV sets were unaffordable for the vast majority and according to Broadcasters' Audience Research Board (BARB) statistics, in 1956 two-thirds of homes did not have a TV set.[11]

Freda Lingstrom, hailed as the pioneer of children's TV output, took charge of the BBC children's department from 1951–6. Her vision was in keeping with the BBC's core principles to inform, educate, and entertain. She developed the *Watch with Mother* strand (1953–75), bringing a number of classic children's TV shows to our screens such as *Andy Pandy* (1950–9), a stripy-playsuit-wearing puppet who encouraged toddlers watching at home to join in with his songs and dance routines, and *The Flowerpot Men* (1952–4) featuring the cheeky characters Bill and Ben. Both were brought back to life in the 2000s with stop-motion animation replacing the original puppet strings. During her expansive career at the BBC Lingstrom commissioned cult studio variety show *Crackerjack* (1955–84), renowned for being filmed in front of an energetic audience of children, and *The Sooty Show* (BBC, 1955–67, ITV, 1968–92), one of the longest-running children's programmes, featuring the yellow bear glove puppet. It has returned to the screen in various guises since its inception, most recently reimagined for the twenty-first-century generation by ITV in 2011.

The BBC dominated children's content until the arrival of the commercial channel ITV in 1955. ITV's remit was to entertain; it had big budgets and imported popular US shows such as *Lassie* (1954–73) alongside producing original family drama such as *The Adventures of Robin Hood* (1955–9).

Since the 1950s the BBC and ITV have been competing against one another for ratings. The BBC brought us *Doctor Who* in 1963 and ITV brought us *Thunderbirds* in 1964. Both were huge successes and their appeal lives on at home and internationally. A revamped CGI version of *Thunderbirds* began in 2015 on ITV, and *Doctor Who* rebooted in 2005 for a new generation and continues to receive high audience ratings. These shows are tried-and-tested formats and TV companies often consider them less risky than investing in original content. The revived versions make financial sense to TV companies because they already have a successful track record of engaging audiences and a trusted brand identity that has the potential to reach global audiences and bring in big bucks through additional merchandising revenue. They also appeal to nostalgic parents who are happy to introduce their children to new versions of the shows they enjoyed watching in their childhood.

Scheduling

The children's TV landscape has completely changed. In 1954 there was just one hour a day but this has gradually increased throughout the decades. Live studio entertainment formats dominated the Saturday morning schedules from the 1970s to the 1990s, with the BBC and ITV going head-to-head to win audiences. Prior to this there had been a few Saturday morning cartoons but not an entire morning dedicated to children. The channel-defining shows that marked each decade started with *Multi-Coloured Swap Shop* (BBC, 1976–82), responsible for the first TV phone-in and *Tiswas* (ATV, 1974–82), which was more chaotic and messy with baked bean and pie-slinging, setting the theme for later Saturday morning TV shows *Going Live!* (BBC, 1987–93), *Live and Kicking* (BBC, 1993–2001) and *SM:TV Live* (ITV, 1998–2003). The classic Saturday morning show typically followed a magazine format with three hours of chat, phone-ins, games, celebrity guests, music, comedy and cartoons, and the appeal of these shows was their spontaneous and anarchic spirit. In the 2000s their popularity started to wane with increasing competition for viewing figures, caused by fragmented viewing habits and a greater choice of dedicated, round-the-clock children's TV channels for every age group from babies and preschoolers to tweens and teens.

In the 1990s satellite children's channels such as Nickelodeon and Disney arrived in the UK, competing with BBC and ITV for viewers. As well as having main channels, they also offered additional content for specific demographics; Nick Jr. for the under six-year-olds, Nicktoons for cartoons, Disney Junior for under five-year-olds, and the gender-skewed Disney XD, for boys aged 6–14. The BBC launched two dedicated children's channels (CBBC for 6- to 12-year-olds and CBeebies for preschoolers in 2002) and ITV launched its CiTV channel in 2006. Baby TV was the first channel aimed solely at babies and channels such as Pop, Nickelodeon and the Cartoon Network started offering a 24-hour service with programmes aired throughout the day.

Blue Peter (1958–), a topical magazine format, is the longest-running children's TV show in the world. How has it survived in the increasingly competitive world of children's TV? One of the key aspects is that it regularly freshens the series with new presenting talent. The presenters are the face of the show and are carefully selected to reflect changing times and to meet its audience needs. The first *Blue Peter* presenters were middle-class, and dressed formally. Gradually presenters have relaxed their appearance to appear more accessible to children. In an effort to better represent audience diversity, John Noakes became the first presenter with a regional accent in 1965, and the first black presenter was Diane-Louise Jordan in 1990.

The show has regular facelifts to its set, logo and music to keep up to date and strives to engage its audience, maintain high-quality production values and keep pace with technological advances while remaining true to the original concept.

Key Ingredients

Many children's TV programmes include children at the heart of the programme as actors, contributors or presenters, so how do you go about working with children and getting the best out of them?

First, know your audience. Often in children's TV you cast older children who look younger as this makes directing easier. So in Cbeebies drama *Topsy and Tim*, young-looking eight-year-olds play five-year-olds and on preschool VTs the kids filmed are typically five or six, rather than two or three, so that they have a better understanding of what you want to achieve and also don't get tired so quickly.

It is important to choose any children that you want to work with carefully. Not everyone is made for TV and you want to avoid working with disinterested or painfully shy kids. Everybody can be a bit nervous but you are looking for children who have a lot of energy and personality, and come alive on-screen. It is also helpful if they are easy to be around rather than difficult or stroppy. Kids can also feel a lot more self-conscious if they are in earshot of their parents or have legions of extras looking over them, so bear this in mind.

Dramas have auditions to find new talent and typically go through acting schools or agents, but to find great contributors for a game show or entertainment show it is often best to go to ordinary schools throughout the country so that you get a good range of diversity. You should seek permission by contacting the local authority first and then the school and ask them to select interested, lively, confident children for you to meet. There is no point in meeting a whole class, as some kids will not be keen to be involved. Always allow enough time to do this, as permission needs to be granted by parents and guardians.

Foster great relationships with a few local schools and involve them in the programme-making process. During the development stage it is important to find out what your audience thinks about the idea. Making a taster or sizzle and recording children's opinions helps to bring an idea to life and helps a commissioner to see its value. If you're making a game show, test it out on the appropriately aged kids. Are they engaged? Would they want to watch it? Do they have suggestions to make that would improve the format?

If you are involving children in your programme then you and your team need to have a Disclosure and Barring Service (DBS) check (previously known as a CRB check). Any child under the age of 16 needs a licence from their local authority to take part in filming. If filming is going to take longer than one day it is wise to arrange your shoot over a weekend or during school holidays. There is a range of measures that you have to adhere to when working with children, and it is important that they have regular breaks and cannot work for more than a certain number of hours in a day. They must also be chaperoned on set at all times. For further details about working with children, seek advice from the child's local authority.

Know your channel. In contrast to BBC children's programmes, Channel 4, with its remit to offer something different and edgier, brought us *Wise Up*. What works on one channel won't work on another. *Wise Up* shook up children's TV by featuring gobby, opinionated working-class kids challenging adults and authority figures by going undercover to tackle issues that concerned them – from ice cream vans selling cigarettes to underage kids, to interviewing the commissioner of the Metropolitan Police about racism in the police force. The series went on to win multiple Emmys, BAFTAs and RTS Awards, and helped pave the way for *Nick News*, a rival children's news offering to BBC's *Newsround*, with kids as the reporters, bringing the news stories that mattered to them with the slogan, 'watch it, cos you're on it.'

New technology offers exciting challenges for programme-makers and you need to embrace it. Children are still watching TV even though there are so many other things vying for their attention. The internet has changed the way children consume TV and interactivity and online content is hugely important in children's TV. Today's children have grown up in the digital age. It is harder than ever for TV producers to gain their attention so you need to be inventive and experiment with new ways of doing things. Green screen and blue screen are easily accessible now, so see what interesting worlds and backdrops you can create. Kids are early adapters to new formats so it's essential for children's programmes to be forward-facing. TV has to meet the emerging habits of its users and find new ways to engage with kids in the digital age but maintain standards. Have fun with new technology but remember you also need good stories and casting for your progamme to fly!

Children's TV Case Study: *Teletubbies*

Teletubbies was first broadcast in the UK on the BBC in 1997 and its 365 episodes ran until 1999. The original series was co-created by Anne Wood of Ragdoll Productions and artist and writer Andrew Davenport. It became a huge global success and was translated into 45 languages, making it one of the BBC's most lucrative programmes.

Image 9 *Teletubbies* – monitor (Courtesy of Darrall Macqueen Ltd)

A reversioned series of *Teletubbies* was commissioned by the BBC's preschool channel Cbeebies in 2014, with Nickelodeon picking up US broadcast and on-demand rights to the brand-new 60 × 12' series for its Nick Jr. channel. There were 60 new episodes in 2015. It was filmed in Twickenham studios in London, instead of its original location in Warwickshire, with the Teletubby landscape replaced and replicated by a detailed model that was enhanced via CGI. It features the original costumed characters Po, Laa-Laa, Dipsy and Tinky Winky, and uses state-of-the-art camera technology and post-production to update it for a new audience but retain all of the charm of the original iconic series. Director of Photography of *Teletubbies* Simon Reay, who also worked on the original version, explains the importance of technology on the revamped series:

> New technology was vital; this was shot on Red Epic 4K and 5K res for all the blue screen work and for capturing all the model work, and we wanted to shoot high-resolution because there is a lot of compositing, visual effects going on and that benefits from the highest resolution you can possibly achieve. We are using classic photography techniques, and bringing them right up to date, using a real model. Our world is real, our characters are real, and all the other little bits are CG, so that is nice, bringing old technology back to the forefront and going, 'right let's do this!' You can see why people get excited about CGI, and aren't we clever and we've created something that

isn't real and put it onto a computer – like a dinosaur. Brilliant, that is great, but it was lovely to bring this back to old classic techniques, which complemented perfectly with *Teletubbies* which is all real to start with, so to have a fully CG *Teletubbies* would have been completely wrong so it is lovely that our set was real, albeit 20 times smaller than the original set!

Teletubbies caused quite a stir when it first aired. It broke the rules, changing the way children's TV was made. It was hailed as a revolutionary preschool format and caused controversy over the teletubbies' 'baby' language and the fact that their theme song is 'Teletubbies say eh oh' instead of 'hello', leading some to worry that it would be harmful to children's speech and development.

Image 10 *Teletubbies* – blue screen (Courtesy of Darrall Macqueen Ltd)

Behind the Scenes – The Big Interview with Maddy Darrall

Maddy Darrall is Executive Producer of *Teletubbies* and co-owner of Darrall Macqueen, the independent production company behind reversion of *Teletubbies*.

Why has *Teletubbies* been revamped?

When we were first approached by DHX Media, who now own the rights to the series, we were very reticent about becoming involved because obviously it was an incredible, groundbreaking series and it has gone on to be iconic globally and it felt to us as a company that there was a huge amount of risk in trying to remake something that, if you didn't have to you wouldn't touch. Nothing needed fixing so we had a lot of conversations before we agreed to go ahead, asking 'why is it being remade?' *Teletubbies* is getting on for 20 years old, and it was shot on standard definition and nowadays globally all broadcasters want HD shows and that was a clear reason why this show had to be remade. We did go through a dialogue whether there was a way to up-res the series because there is so little about the original series that you would want to tinker with, and that wasn't possible. We were very clear from day one that we love the series as it currently is, and that creatively we wanted to stay as true as possible to the original thinking behind the series.

What was the commissioning process?

DHX Media invested in a pilot. Children's TV pilots do not go hand in hand any more but with *Teletubbies* we had to get it right from day one, so they invested in a test shoot. We built a model, brought the original Laa-Laa costume out of storage, found a performance artist and filmed various sequences on blue screens with miniature mounds and composited the two together. We introduced in this process a visual effects company called Lola to pull off the CG work. The series was created in a very high-tech way but when anybody watche[d] it, I didn't want them to watch it and think, 'oh gosh I can see where the CG is!' I wanted them to think, 'how on earth is that character walking around in that landscape?' Once Lola were on board and they had achieved a wonderful test scene it gave everybody the confidence to make it work. Cbeebies saw how we were envisaging it and heard about some of the new elements that we wanted to bring to it and quite quickly said yes, which gave us our first broadcaster, and Nickelodeon in the US commissioned it which is brilliant news as they are the main children's broadcaster in the US.

How does this version differ from the original?

There was no hesitation in our minds that the characters would not be CGI; as is the case in many remakes, this didn't feel appropriate. In the original series they couldn't always shoot outside because of the elements, and actually looking back on the 365 episodes, there is an awful lot that is filmed inside and we knew we couldn't do that these days, we can't start with a schedule and then just change it because it has just rained because we have to have control over it. We hope we have given *Teletubbies* a feeling that this has been revived and regenerated for a new generation but is true to the original series.

The key to the development process was that myself and our script editor painstakingly watched the 365 original episodes, and read through all the original scripts, and worked quite closely with an educational adviser to create the 60 new episodes. Scripting was a long process.

We have changed very little but made some visual enhancements and now Teletubbyland features flowers and trees that can grow and an eco-friendly windmill. From speaking to the original crew we lost impractical elements such as the slide that was very difficult for a heavy Teletubby to use.

The new reversion of *Teletubbies* is 15 minutes in length (12 minutes for international, that suits their schedules better) and the original series was 28 minutes. The episodes were often hugely beautifully orchestrated but had very protracted scenes of falling over, and standing and so on, so what we realised quite quickly is that by the time we had created an opening and closing, and the tummy tales, location VTs with children in the outside world, we actually had very little time to do long, protracted scenes so we started to drill down what the core of the series is. Without a good script and without really getting under the skin of the script, you can have all the visual thinking in the world but the show won't really resonate with the audience. It was so vitally important that we made sure that we kept what was so wonderful about the series originally, and made sure that we didn't change it too dramatically from what it was originally and that it was funny.

We have given the interior a very different world, it was a very purple-blue-pink colour which I think in the 1990s was probably very *de rigueur* and it would not really feel like it now, but it is funny how many people walked onto the set when we were filming and didn't notice that it was different, yet it is just like the original dome! The shape was there and the characters were the same, and everything around it felt the same. So really a lot of those choices, which I hope will just pass viewers by, were painstakingly thought out, to make sure that we were making 60 episodes of something that the audience really care about.

We have introduced a tubby custard ride and whenever the machine has run out of custard, which is often, it gives us the wonderful pleasure of seeing them running around on a custard ride and there are versions of it that are very messy, there are versions of it where there are bubbles everywhere. That is one of the new elements that I think will be very interesting. The tubby phone is new too, we wanted to bring some sort of technology into it; technological toys are very relevant to children's lives and the teletubbies now have touchscreen tummies.

The same song remains, we have got different voice artists and the BBC Philharmonic have recorded the music; it feels very big and grand because you have got this full orchestra playing the iconic *Teletubbies* music. Part of the joy of *Teletubbies* is you never know what will happen, it is not formulaic, you know there will be an opening and closing but even with that you never know which Teletubby is going to say goodbye, so we have made ourselves true to the essence of the original. The formula is no formula!

Tell me about the casting?

Casting for the teletubbies [themselves] is absolutely vital. It is a physical job running around on these domes and they have got to have good core strength to not fall over in those costumes. We saw quite a lot of people and were looking for people who can bring these costumes to life and make a performance pop. A few of the teletubbies were also in *The Night Garden*; their experience really shone out during the auditions.

In terms of voice talent, the narrator, Daniel [Rigby], is just wonderful, he nails every single scene and that's important, because if we got that wrong, you would have kept hearing it, and now you don't hear it, you just think that was beautiful. I really liked the idea that our narrator was not such a well-known voice; it just felt really right to me. There is obviously always a need with these sorts of big global productions to have some PR-friendly voices attached too, and Jane Horrocks was someone we talked about very early on, giving the Teletubby phone a bit of character, and then Jim Broadbent and Fearne Cotton said yes which was wonderful.

Image 11 *Teletubbies* – clapper board (Courtesy of Darrall Macqueen Ltd)

What is the schedule?

Our day starts at eight o'clock on camera, but we wouldn't get the Teletubby performers until 9:30 every day because it is a very strenuous occupation being inside a Teletubby costume; these are not people like in a Disney theme park that wave a bit and give the odd cuddle. It's strenuous work! They come with quite a large entourage because each Teletubby needs a couple of minders and dressers. We have two sets of costumes and two sets of heads, making sure that everything works properly on the Teletubbies. Many people try to persuade me that they should be using animatronics because that's the era we are now in, but we have stuck with the original mechanics that the Teletubbies had; it is basically a cable in each hand, one does the mouth, one does the eyes, it is really low-tech but I think it is very successful for communicating with the young audience. The first thing that the Teletubby performers do is come onto the set for a rehearsal, not in costume, but wearing helmets. This shows the camera team the height and dimensions of the aerial for their frame. It's important to spend time before we put the cameras on doing a thorough block-through. This is time well spent as once the cameras are on there is quite a lot of pressure to shoot a scene quickly and efficiently, and not to waste time, so an awful lot of planning goes into that because the Teletubby performers need breaks every 5–20 minutes depending on the scene. [You] always have that pressure on you that you need that shot in the 20-minute window. We usually do on average three or four scenes a day but if it's a really taxing scene, I mean strenuous for them, and has a lot of technical working out it could take a whole day to film one sequence. You know it is not fast and it takes time to get it right. They finish around six o'clock, studio crew not until seven.

Who works on *Teletubbies*?

On the production team side, we have a series producer and a director who are very focused on what goes on in the studio, and then we have a separate team for the Teletubby tales that consists of a producer and directors and researchers and their own co-ordinator and secretary and runner looking after all the locations, working with children, getting inserts.

Then you have your studio unit that really is the producer and the director, and you have edit producers as well, who start on the material as it comes through and then a big behind-the-scenes logistics team. [We also have] our head of production, production manager, co-ordinator, secretary [and] a couple of runners, and it takes that level of people to make a big beast like this work for six months. Our camera team consists of DOP, camera operator, first AD, second AD, a digital imaging technician (DIT), two grips, a gaffer, two electricians and a rigger.

We have got the benefit of recording all this technical stuff with no challenge with sound because we re-record all the voices later down the line, so part of our protracted post-production schedule is all the re-recording of the audio. The costumed characters have guide tracks on the studio floor, which is really crucial, so we have somebody there who is picking up all the audio and all the artists come in later down the line and we record all the audio all over again.

We have also got a script supervisor who is vital on a job like this, getting all that complicated information down and making detailed notes for the visual effects team and for the edit. If those notes aren't totally clear, we are going to waste so much time and no one will remember, so that is a vital role.

What is the future of children's TV?
I feel very optimistic about the future of children's television. I think what is starting to happen now, because of the way in which children can access shows on multiplatforms, on iPlayer and via YouTube from all over the world, they are making their own schedules and actually on a domestic level that is great because they are not reliant on a normal schedule that somebody has decided is the right order for them to watch things in. Globally, what is starting to happen is that a lot of the UK shows are becoming even more watched. I think we have got an incredible reputation in this country for really great children's storymakers. We have so many iconic children's brands that have been global successes, and I think the climate is just getting right and now people globally are able to say, 'gosh if there is British content available for children, we know it will be good and we would like it' and I feel really optimistic that we are in quite good shape. There are some really exciting opportunities globally to get more programmes out there and your shows watched by perhaps more people than when there was that gatekeeper commissioner who may have decided that children wouldn't like a certain show. I think now children are going to be able to access what they want and it is only going to be good for British products.

Summary

▸ You need a really good script to make a children's TV show come alive. If it doesn't work on the page, it won't work on-screen.
▸ Match your casting needs with the audience and don't underestimate the importance of finding good performers.

- Remember to do a thorough block-through before you turn the camera on – a useful tip in all genres but particularly important when working with children or performers in heavy costumes.
- Know your audience. It's not good enough to say it's a children's show, so be specific, whether it's for babies, toddlers or tweens, you need to know this to connect with the viewer.
- Experiment with new technology to push the boundaries of what you can achieve.

Insider Knowledge

The saying goes that you should never work with children or animals. It can be chaotic and it's always surprising. The best advice when working with kids is to think creatively and be patient. There is a knack to directing children. You really want them to forget that the camera is there so that they will relax and enjoy themselves. Do rehearsals and record them, as sometimes these can be the most natural performances. There is no point getting cross with kids. If they're not getting their lines right, don't make them do it over and over again. Take a break. Reassure them, respect them and listen to them – something might be on their mind. You won't get the performance that you want by laying on the pressure, so make it fun! And always have snacks to hand!

Now Try This

1. Practise with the *Teletubbies* script and then make your own version.
2. Watch old episodes of children's TV programmes (many are accessible on YouTube and similar channels or via the British Film Institute (BFI)). Are there any that could be

revamped for a new generation to enjoy? Re-work the original without losing its spirit – remember to consider the style, script, cast, crew, audience, budget and schedule.
3. Now turn your idea into a taster.

Sample Shooting Script: *Teletubbies*

SCENE 1 – GENERIC OPENING TITLES

SHOT 1

THE SUN RISES OVER TELETUBBYLAND. THE BABY IN THE SUN LOOKS DOWN AND GIGGLES.

A RABBIT EMERGES FROM ITS BURROW AND SNIFFS THE AIR.

THE SUN'S RAYS BURN THROUGH TO THE NEXT SHOT....

SHOT 2

THE CAMERA TRACKS ACROSS THE GRASS TOWARDS THE BROW OF A HILL. A FEW FLOWERS BEGIN TO TURN THEIR HEADS TOWARDS THE HILL.

FEMALE NARRTOR   1

Over the hills and far away, Teletubbies come to play.

AS THE CAMERA CONTINUES ITS TRACK TOWARDS IT, THE TELETUBBIES START TO POP OUT OF THE TOP OF HOME HILL. THE CAMERA SETTLES.

MALE NARRATOR   2

One.

TINKY WINKY POPS OUT OF HOME HILL.

TINKY WINKY   3

One.

MALE NARRATOR   4

Two.

LAA-LAA POPS OUT OF HOME HILL.

LAA-LAA   5

Two.

MALE NARRATOR   6

Three.

PO POPS OUT OF HOME HILL.

PO 7

Three.

MALE NARRATOR 8

Four.

SHORT PAUSE.
DIPSY POPS OUT OF HOME HILL.

DIPSY 9

Four.

IN FRONT OF THE 4-SHOT OF THE TELETUBBIES, LOGO/LETTERS EXPAND
TO SPELL 'TELETUBBIES'.

MALE ANNOUNCER 10

Teletubbies!

SHOT 3

[THEME MUSIC BEGINS]

CRANE SHOT FROM ABOVE. THE TELETUBBIES RUN DOWN THE DOME
OF HOME HILL TOWARDS THE CAMERA AND UP THE OPPOSITE HILL.
FLOWERS BLOOM IN THEIR WAKE AND RABBITS HOP ON THE HILL.

SHOT 4

THE TELETUBBIES HAVE CRESTED THE HILL AND ARE NOW RUNNING
TOWARDS THE LENS.

THE CAMERA TRACKS BACK BETWEEN THE HILLOCKS AS VOICE
TRUMPETS EMERGE.

VOICE TRUMPETS 11

Time for Teletubbies

Time for Teletubbies

(tbc)

[Time for Teletubbies Time for Teletubbies]

FLOWERS CONTINUE TO BLOOM.

CUT TO:

SHOT 5

SINGLE TINKY WINKY ON A HILLOCK DANCING WITH HIS SIGNATURE
MOVE.

MALE NARRATOR 12

Tinky Winky

TINKY WINKY 13
Tinky Winky
CUT TO:

SHOT 6
SINGLE DIPSY ON A HILLOCK DANCING WITH HIS SIGNATURE MOVE.

MALE NARRATOR 14
Dipsy

DIPSY 15
Dipsy
CUT TO:

SHOT 7
SINGLE LAA-LAAON A HILLOCK DANCING WITH HER SIGNATURE MOVE.

MALE NARRATOR 16
Laa-Laa

LAA-LAA 17
Laa-Laa
CUT TO:

SHOT 8
SINGLE PO ON A HILLOCK DANCING WITH HER SIGNATURE MOVE.

MALE NARRATOR 18
Po

PO 19
Po
CUT TO:

SHOT 9
CRANE SHOT ABOVE.
AS THE CAMERA CRANES DOWN THE TELETUBBIES WALK ONE BEHIND
THE OTHER ACROSS FRAME.
WALK ONE BEHIND THE OTHER OVER THE HILLS AND BACK (SPEEDED UP).

MALE NARRATOR 20
Teletubbies

ALL TELETUBBIES 21
Teletubbies
THE TELETUBBIES CLEAR FRAME.

MALE NARRATOR 22

Say hello!

BEAT

TELETUBBIES CLOSE TO CAMERA, WAVING.

ALL TELETUBBIES 23

Eh-oh!

(+Big Hug for international)

SHOT 10 (Not in international version)

TINKY WINKY AND DIPSY TUMMY BUMP AND DANCE ON A HILLOCK. BEHIND THEM A TREE BLOSSOMS. [NB/ NOT IN INTERNATIONAL VERSION]

MALE NARRATOR 24

Tinky Winky, Dipsy...

SHOT 11 (Not in international version)

LAA-LAA AND PO TUMMY BUMP AND GIGGLE ON A HILLOCK. BEHIND THEM A TREE BLOSSOMS. [NB/ NOT IN INTERNATIONAL VERSION]

MALE NARRATOR 25

Laa-Laa, Po.

CUT TO REVEAL ....

SHOT 12 (Not in international version) THE TWO SETS OF TELETUBBIES (TINKY WINKY & DIPSY, LAA-LAA & PO) ON ADJACENT HILLOCKS.

MALE NARRATOR {CONT'D} 26

Teletubbies

THE TELETUBBIES NOW RUN AND SKIP TOWARDS LENS AS THE CAMERA TRACKS BACK TO REVEAL A FOREGROUND HILLOCK.

THE TELETUBBIES CLIMB THE HILLOCK.

ALL TELETUBBIES 27

Big hug!

AS THE TELETUBBIES HUG, FLOWERS BLOOM ON THE GROUND AROUND THEM.

ALL TELETUBBIES (CONT'D) 28

Ah.

SHOT 13 29

CUT TO WINDMILL. AS THE WINDMILL SPINS AND GLITTER.

SHOT 14

THIS IS SHOT 12 CONTINUED. SHOT 9 CONTINUED FOR INTERNATIONAL.

ALL TELETUBBIES   30

Uh-oh!

THE TUBBIES RUN AWAY FROM CAMERA (SPEEDED UP) OVER HILLS.
VOICE TRUMPET RISES UP CLOSE TO LENS.

VOICE TRUMPET   31

Where have the Teletubbies gone?

SHOT 15

FULL FRAME SUN & BABY. THE BABY MAKES A LITTLE NOISE.

SHOT 16

VARIOUS VIEWS OF HOME HILL AND RABBITS
(10 DIFFERENT COMBINATIONS)
                                                                        CUT TO:

SCENE 2 - EXT. HILLS

VIEW OF HILLS

ALL FOUR TELETUBBIES WALK IN LINE ON TO A HILL. THEY STAND IN
A LINE. RABBITS RUN PAST.

ALL TELETUBBIES   32

Eh-oh!

MALE NARRATOR   33

One day in Teletubbyland, the Teletubbies were saying hello.

TINKY WINKY   34

Teletubbies saying 'eh oh'.

DIPSY   35

...say 'eh-oh'.

LAA-LAA   36

Sayin' 'eh-oh'.

PO   37

Eh-oh!

MALE NARRATOR   38

First Tinky Winky said hello to Dipsy.
TINKY WINKY TURNS TO HIS LEFT TO DIPSY.

TINKY WINKY   39

Eh-oh Dipsy.

DIPSY 40

Eh-oh Tinky Winky.

THEY BELLY BUMP AND BOTTOM BUMP, GIGGLE.

TINKY WINKY 41

Big hug. THEY HUG.

DIPSY 42

Big hug!

THE TELETUBBIES LOOK TO CAM.

MALE NARRATOR 43

Then Dipsy said hello to Laa-Laa.

DIPSY TURNS TO HIS LEFT TO LAA-LAA.

DIPSY 44

Eh-oh Laa-Laa.

LAA-LAA 45

Eh-oh Dipsy.

THEY BELLY BUMP AND BOTTOM BUMP, GIGGLE.

DIPSY 46

Big hug. THEY HUG.

LAA-LAA 47

Big hug!

THE TELETUBBIES LOOK TO CAM.

MALE NARRATOR 48

Laa-Laa said hello to Po.

LAA-LAA TURNS TO HER LEFT TO PO.

LAA-LAA 49

Eh-oh Po.

PO 50

Eh-oh Laa-Laa.

THEY BELLY BUMP AND BOTTOM BUMP, GIGGLE.

LAA-LAA 51

Big hug.

THEY HUG.

PO   52

Big hug!
THE TELETUBBIES LOOK TO CAM. PO TURNS TO HER LEFT. NOTHING
THERE.

MALE NARRATOR   53

But there was no one for Po to say hello to ....

PO   54

No one Po eh-oh.

ALL TELETUBBIES   55

(Giggles)

PO   56

Po say eh-oh?
PO NUDGES LAA-LAA.

PO (CONT'D)   57

No one Po eh-oh.
LAA-LAA NUDGES DIPSY.

LAA-LAA   58

No one Po eh-oh.
DIPSY NUDGES TINKY WINKY.

DIPSY   59

No one Po eh-oh.
TINKY WINKY THINKS THEN WALKS ALONG IN FRONT OF THE OTHERS
AND STANDS IN LINE NEXT TO PO GIGGLING AS HE GOES.
TINKY WINKY TAPS PO ON THE SHOULDER. PO TURNS TO THE LEFT TO
LOOK AT HIM. SHE LOOKS SURPRISED.

PO   60

Eh-oh Tinky Winky.

TINKY WINKY   61

Eh-oh Po.
PO GIGGLES EXCITEDLY, LOOKS TO CAM
[PO SMILES].
TINKY WINKY AND PO BELLY BUMP, BOTTOM BUMP, GIGGLING.

PO 62

Big hug!

TINKY WINKY AND PO HUG. ALL AROUND THEM, FLOWERS MAGICALLY BLOOM.

PO (CONT'D) 63

Big hug.

THEY ALL DO A BIG GROUP HUG.

ALL TELETUBBIES 64

Aaaaaah/big hug.

SFX WINDMILL. TUBBIES REACT.

ALL TELETUBBIES (CONT'D) 65

Uh-oh.

TELETUBBIES EXIT/RUN. WINDMILL WHIZZES ROUND.
                                    CUT TO:

12

TALK SHOWS AND MAGAZINE FORMATS

A talk show or chat show is a genre in which a group of people discuss various topics put forth by the host. Shows that typify this conversational approach are ITV's *Loose Women* and US equivalent version *The View*, featuring celebrity women with strong opinions on the issues of the day. Talk shows can also involve ordinary people with extraordinary stories, again led by the presenter but can involve more interaction from a studio audience, shows like *Jeremy Kyle* and *Jerry Springer*.

Late-night talk shows led by a big showbiz name feature interviews with high-profile celebrity guests who talk about their work and personal lives as well as promoting their latest films, television shows, music and books. The hosts are often comedians who the show is named after, such as Graham Norton, Alan Carr and Jonathan Ross, and Jay Leno and Jimmy Fallon are big-name hosts in the USA.

Magazine shows, as the name suggests, are programmes with a variety of different items, from news, VT inserts, music, fashion and everything in between. As seen in previous chapters the running order is key, with the studio gallery carefully keeping the show's hosts on track to move seamlessly between items. Shows like ITV's *This Morning* and the BBC's motoring show *Top Gear* are all examples of this.

Studio magazine shows are typically the main vehicle for breakfast television, with a combination of news bulletins, interviews and reports. Broadcast on our screens between 6 and 9.30am, they have a mixed target audience of parents, pensioners and people getting ready for work. So the show needs clever scheduling to satisfy these different audience needs. Often the same item is repeated multiple times as the viewers are only watching for a few minutes a time in between getting in the shower, getting children to brush their teeth and running out the door. Hence lots of use of stings, which are quick bursts of music and graphics that punctuate items and wake the audience up at home. There is always a clock in the corner of the screen as time is of the essence in the morning for the busy household.

Much of the success is attributed to the talent driving these shows. Broadcasters will spend vast amounts to secure talent that fits their brand values and often will poach from other channels to achieve this – Graham Norton from Channel 4 to BBC and Susannah Reid from BBC to ITV. Talk shows tend to have one main host that fronts the show. Breakfast TV tends to have a double act or a team of hosts that rely on chemistry to kick-start your day. Graham Sherrington worked on the global format hit *Top Gear*. Here, he explains the importance of talent:

> Every job that I go for, pretty much, every kind of TV exec that I bump into, they always ask why was the original *Top Gear* so successful? I think the key was the chemistry between the presenters. But there are some other elements that distinguished it from other mainstream magazine formats that made it popular to watch. It caused controversy and not intentionally, all the time, because the views were very direct, and it's incredible production values. The films … about the races and the power tests almost have filmic qualities and it hadn't really been done before. So you add that to a mix of studio environment, which really grew. I would say those ingredients together, the presenters' chemistry and the great production values made it a hit.

Brief History of Talk Shows and Magazine Formats

Breakfast TV

Breakfast television launched much earlier in the USA in 1952 with the *Today* show, compared to the UK, which was not until the 1980s. British breakfast television first trialled on the regional ITV station Yorkshire Television for a six-week run, before the Independent Broadcasting Authority created an entire franchise for the genre, awarded to TV-am. Launch delays for TV-am gave the BBC the chance to get its own morning programme on-air first. In 1993,

GMTV out-bid TV-am to win the franchise, later reverting back to ITV Breakfast Broadcasting Limited. The new era launched with *Daybreak* and *Lorraine* in September 2010, and was later revamped and replaced by *Good Morning Britain* in April 2014.

Over the years Channel 4 attempted to break the dominance of BBC and ITV, with irreverent formats skewed for younger audiences like 1992's *The Big Breakfast,* presented by Chris Evans, referred to as groundbreaking. It included handheld cameras, sexy interviews on the bed with Paula Yates and always a sense that there was a party going on. The show ran for a decade but could not sustain the high ratings of the earlier years. Later came *RI:SE*, but it was never as successful as *The Big Breakfast.* With falling ratings for Channel 4's breakfast audience, they returned to screening US imported dramas in the slot.

The race to win the breakfast audience is a hotly contested one. It is seen as an important battleground by the broadcasters, who believe if they can win the morning audience they may be able get them to stay for the rest of the day.

Talk Shows

NBC's *The Tonight Show* is the world's longest-running talk show, which began broadcasting in 1954 and is still around today. The first host was Steve Allen, who took much of his style from his previous late-night radio show. Allen is widely credited as developing the late-night TV talk show's format with conventions such as the presenter's opening comical spiel, celebrity interviews, comedy, music and studio audience banter. Late-night talk shows remain ratings winners worldwide with US shows such as *The Tonight Show starring Jimmy Fallon* and *Late Show with David Letterman* leading the pack.

In terms of the daily talk show *The Oprah Winfrey Show* is seen as one of the most influential. The show began in 1986 and became one of the longest-running tabloid talk shows in the world. Originally championing the voice of ordinary people with real stories, Oprah Winfrey became a real talking point. Oprah Winfrey's success led to a raft of similar talk shows such as *The Jerry Springer Show, Phil Donahue, Sally Jessy Raphael, Geraldo Rivera, Ricki Lake and Montel Williams* all becoming popular daytime juggernauts. The

UK followed suit with their own, initially tamer, versions such as *Vanessa, Jerry Springer UK* and later *Trisha* and *Jeremy Kyle*.

Key Ingredients

Although talk shows and magazine shows differ slightly there are many commonalities. The big key to their success is the running order. Often these shows are live, especially breakfast TV shows, so everything is carefully timed to ensure that there will be no dead air. A big part of the producer's job is conceiving ideas, often with the help of hosts, writers and executive producers. Because talk shows are often based on current events or recurring themes in society, the idea-forming portion of a producer's job requires them to be up to date on current events. They might start the day by reading the local and national newspapers or researching trending topics. With a show topic in mind, the producer will seek out show guests and book them into time slots on the show.

Lisa Armstrong, TV series producer working on such shows as ITV's *This Morning, Lorraine* and *Jerry Springer UK*, and now based in Dubai, says:

> The daily routine of going through a magazine show is basically you start by going through everything. Most places have a diary or a forward-planning area. If you don't, it's basically about making sure that you're across everything going on locally, or internationally as well. So if it's a particularly big day, for example Band-Aid has released their new single today and it's had so many hits already on iTunes, you need to know. Then it is going through newspapers, very often now it is also going through social media – at the moment I get a lot of stories from Facebook and Twitter.

For television you need visuals. For morning and evening they need bitesized chunks. So, it needs to be short, snappy, and everything needs to be in chunks of five minutes. Maximum. You need to make sure that your guests are eloquent, and that they are not going to stumble. And also, that they know what they are talking about and they are well briefed. You may think that on paper they are great guests, but ultimately they need to talk. Whether it is radio or TV, you need to get out of them what you think you are going to get.

Having identified stories you want to use it is then about carefully working out timings. If you know you have a three-hour breakfast show to fill you will have some fixed elements within that, for example the top of the hour and every half hour will include the news and weather. Your show will need to open with a 'coming up' menu, then you may want to move between items, with a range from harder-hitting news to a human interest story. Here is an example to consider:

6am	News and weather
	Item 1
	Item 2
	Item 3
6.30am	News and weather
	Item 4
	Item 5
	Item 6
7am	News and weather
	Repeat stories from first hour with a slightly different nuance

In hours two and three of the show you may want to repeat your stories from the first hour with a slightly different angle – remember the audience is constantly changing in this part of the day as they are getting ready for work and school. The job of producing a TV talk show involves a lot of hard work and careful attention to detail. Among their daily duties, talk show producers book guests and celebrities, plan the running order of items, prepare the presenter's script, research contributor background notes, film inserts for the main show and write captions that will appear on the screen to identify contributors.

Neil Thompson, editor of *Good Morning Britain*, explains the key ingredients for a successful breakfast show:

> It's a world into which you are waking up, so here is a show that can utterly inform your day, so it's all the news you need, explained, contextualised, and given a hierarchy so you are aware of what is the most important thing you should be aware of that day. It should engage your curiosity by taking care of features, themes [and] lifestyle habits, and representing them to the audience so that they are

excited and their interest is re-engaged or re-tickled by the way in which you have told that story. You have given them talking points, human interest; it is finding those extraordinary stories told by ordinary people – they want to see these people ideally in the studio, on the sofa, talking face-to-face with the presenters.

Often there will be small teams working to produce these shows. The general make-up of a show like that is about three people per show. So you will have a day producer, an assistant producer and a researcher. The team will have sole responsibility for one show per week. Feeding into each dedicated show, you may also have a features team, a news team, a celebrity team and a forward-planning team, feeding stories to all of the day teams as well.

If you are working on a daily talk show typically an hour long, your running order may be governed by commercial breaks (if working on a commercial channel), usually with three parts across an hour with a new story in each segment, as illustrated below:

Pre-titles	
Part One	Story 1
Commercial Break	
Part Two	Story 2
Commercial Break	
Part Three	Story 3
End Credits	

Lisa Armstrong says:

The highest pressure for working on a daily show is ratings! You're only as good as your last show. Nobody really cares that you did a great show ten months ago, they want to know that your show is a ratings number one. Obviously you can have a little small dip, but the minute you start dipping at all, that's when the network's going to start asking 'what are you doing?'

Number two pressure is you tend to cover the same themes all the time: there are probably about six topics. So it's trying to work out how you deliver those stories. It's getting the right hook, for that particular time, and fresh content. Here in Dubai we tend to do roads a lot, health, education and property. The other thing is dealing with how you organise yourself and your day because you're constantly working to a deadline, all the time.

This genre is not for the faint-hearted. You are constantly working to a deadline and often have the added pressure of live television, but it will give you an excellent grounding in the industry with hours of television experience quickly accumulating on your CV.

Case Study: *Good Morning Britain*

Good Morning Britain (GMB) is a breakfast television programme that airs on ITV daily between 6 and 9.25am. As explored in the Key Ingredients section of this chapter, the show is broken down into many items with news being a key fixture to build the schedule around. The first half of the morning programme is typically aimed at those getting ready for work, with a focus on hard news items and traffic reports. Later the programme reflects the changing audience, of housewives and students, with a focus on human interest and entertainment stories. *GMB* is currently presented by main presenters Susanna Reid and Ben Shephard. Their on-screen chemistry and warmth brings a familiar feel to the show. It is shot at the London studios in its own dedicated studio five days a week. The team is 250-strong and it is a big operation to achieve just under 20 hours of television every week.

Behind the Scenes with *Good Morning Britain*'s Editor Neil Thompson

Neil Thompson is in charge of *GMB*. Before this role, he was a commissioning editor for ITV's factual department, and is a former managing editor for ITV news. He explains the pressures of working on a peak daily show:

> I think the challenge we set ourselves and what I talk about with the team and what we talk about every day is, every day that show has to feel like the team's very first or very last show. It has got to feel compelling and distinctive every single day, so you have to be quite familiar *with* the audience or familiar *for* them so they recognise the presenters, recognise the approach, recognise the opening titles, they know where the news will be, the news bulletins will be, where this programme will be most story-rich in current stories. They also know where the weather will be and they will know where other parts of

furniture will be and within that every single day you will have to surprise them, engage their curiosity through different treatments, different approaches. Often it's very similar stories that we do day in and day out along with other newspapers and broadcasts and news, busy day production outputs.

Image 12 *Good Morning Britain's* series editor Neil Thompson (Courtesy of *TV Times*)

What is the importance of talent in this genre?

It is actually essential – the talent has to [have] and needs a kind of chemistry. You need to have presenters who spark off each other, who would naturally be drawn to each other not necessarily sexually, but sometimes! [You need to have presenters] who are drawn to each other in any environment, so they have an intellectual equality between them and they can answer each other's questions and they can finish each other's sentences before they have finished. [It's] old-fashioned chemistry, they like each other, they respect each other and they can conduct for instance a two-handed inquisition of a challenging interviewee together; they know how to ask an opening question and they can answer and ask a supplementary question.

What is the importance of the studio environment?

That is absolutely key and where we have differed from our predecessors is that we were very keen to build a set that was a place [to] which you came. *GMB* is a place. You are literally on the show as opposed to coming to a series of studio flats that were then dismantled after two-and-a-half hours and replaced by another show. We had the studio designed by a company in New York who have designed studios for CNN, NBC, for ABC, a lot of American networks and some of the UK. We said we wanted a 360 environment, one where you come in and there is a hub, a main desk, from where we open each hour, and we do arc the show so the first hour of the show is a news show, entirely presented from the desk. The second opens at seven at the desk, but then after about 20 minutes we favour the sofa, and the demonstration areas. After eight, we go from being a news show between six and seven, news magazine [between] seven and eight, and a magazine after eight where we entirely favour the sofa. So what was really important was that we had some recognised areas, some we'll use many more times than others; the hub is used a lot, the sofa is used a lot, the demo is used quite a lot with an 80" touchscreen plasma, the performance area is used quite a lot, but specifically rare enough to make you feel special, and the weather presentation area. So those are the key five areas in the studio. The studio has won two very significant awards actually, to our delight, and they were not awards we were even aware we had entered. We won the NABA award for the best news studio outside of the US and also the Sony award as one of the world's best news studios. I think that is fantastic and a great accolade to the instincts that we had about what that place needed to do.

What are the key differences between breakfast television in the UK and the US?

Clearly there is a lot that we have looked at in terms of the US which has helped inform what we have done. It has informed it in a very British way, so at the top of the hour in the States it will be a much faster kind of cut, much faster directed, much pacier opening, [but] we have slowed that down. We use Steadicam in the show, but not as much as in America, because we don't want it to be too whizzy. They want to be able to sit down and settle and watch the show and not feel too discombobulated and not sure what is going on. So the news bulletins may be seven minutes long and we go for a very high story count in those parts of the programme, which we repeat again at the half hour and briefly at the quarter hours. In America that initial bulletin may actually have fewer stories and they probably then fill the remainder of the half hour with slightly more pace. We will go for slightly slower, slightly longer interviews – three-and-a-half minutes long. They might have two-thirds/half of that in the States.

What are the mechanics of making this kind of show?

It is a 24/6 kind of operation. Saturdays are staffed but a very small staff because that is one day we don't have a show the next day, so we have a bit of a lie in! Sunday we have no show but we have a show on Monday, so effectively this will be up and running six days a week with five shows to do, and of course the shift system means that there are people working throughout the 24-hour cycle. You will have a significant number of [the] team who will arrive between 7.30 and 8.30 in the morning, more will arrive at midday, more will arrive at four in the afternoon, more will arrive at 7.30 and 8.30 in the evening and some of them later than that; so we are staggering the shifts, but essentially a large number of people arrive at the beginning of the working day and a large number of people arrive at the end of the working day. We have a number of teams, we have what we call a 'specials' team, who work on those big events, the big strands – it might be an investigation into the dangers online for children, it may be on car seat safety or it might be on just high-street and retail issues anyway. We then have a news planning team who are just working on the news diary and reports of things that might be coming out or strands or investigations we are conducting. Then we have a celebrity desk and they are generating and booking not just guests but also sourcing access to all the red carpet events, or doing the Toronto Film Festival or the Oscars, or just working with our bureau in LA. Then we have an input desk who chase stories of the day.

What is the importance of multiplatform and interactivity?
We have put a lot of time in and go to a lot of trouble to make sure that we source literally thousands of audience reactions every single morning. Someone in the gallery is there just cherry picking, not just emails and texts but also all social media whether it's on Facebook, Twitter, all the interactions, many of which we have called for. Then they have to be assembled by a social media producer. It shows the viewer that there is a link, we are listening and responding.

It is the only part of the television schedule in which you are broadcasting to people who are for a start wearing their undies! It is a very intimate relationship, it is a very chaotic time of the day and in that period you have got to be their friend and able to endlessly engage with them when they are coming out of the shower, for the school run, having lost and then found their briefcase, spilt their cereal, burnt the toast; you are there often utterly engaging them and often in the background, but always basically understanding that if they hear something, they are going to come running and want to see the rest of it. So it is a very intimate relationship and a very busy, demanding time of the day, so you have got to be familiar but you have got to be heard sometimes. You can never afford to be dull or boring which is why, on a daily basis, we go boldly where we've been many times before, about A&E or about the postcode lottery around health, or exam results, or issues around immigration, or you are showing some extraordinary new footage that you have shot or acquired somehow, or telling a story – those stories are often thematically quite familiar but you have got to go about it in a very unfamiliar way to make sure that they understand why they have to listen and watch that day. Within that also you have to know that every now and again, you throw a hand grenade into the millpond and do something very different, and that shows that you are anything but boring.

What is the future of the breakfast show?
It is safe. The reason why I believe it is safe is because you can time shift all sorts of programming, you can time shift your serial dramas, [but] the one thing you can't time shift is the beginning of the day. We are on at the beginning of the day. Now historically, some people ten years ago may have said, and I have occasionally said, the thing about the [breakfast] television [show] is that of course it's vulnerable because why would you need it? Well you need it because it occurs at no other time of the day and at the time of the day when you need that information, you need that mix of warmth, news, relevance, topicality, weather, talking points, the latest insight into breaking stories, what has happened overnight when you haven't been attached [to] your smartphone. You need that and you will only get [that at] the beginning of the day, so in that respect it has a privileged status.

Summary

▸ Talk shows and magazine formats rely on a strong talk show host to drive the programme forward. They skilfully interview guests to get them to reveal exclusive stories. Much of the show's budget will be spent on the talent.

▸ A carefully timed running order will ensure you have enough content in your show, particularly important when a show is live. Always have more items planned than you need, just in case.

▸ As with all programmes, but particularly with a daily/weekly talk show, know your audience well – different day parts will have different people watching your show and your programme needs to reflect this.

▸ The set is important to create the backdrop to these stories. Breakfast TV is usually bright and breezy; talk shows involving people with extraordinary stories may be more muted and have more of a living room feel to develop intimacy; late-night shows will have glitzy lighting – think about your audience and what you are trying to achieve.

Insider Knowledge

Never underestimate how much material you need for a show. Always have a story in reserve should things go wrong. Guests can get stuck in traffic, decide to drop out or not perform as well as you hoped – always have a plan B, C and D!

Now Try This

1. Practise in your own studio with the script for *GMB*. Add camera moves and create camera cards.
2. Access a mix of national news stories from online sources/ newspapers. From the stories of the day create your own running order for a breakfast television show. Think about the channel you are making it for. Do you want it to feel light and breezy or more serious in tone?
3. Write the opening monologue for a late-night chat show. Practise lighting it in a different way from the previous morning show (bright and breezy). Really consider the time of day, the audience and the mood you are trying to create.

Sample Autocue Script: *Good Morning Britain*

WEDNESDAY 15th APRIL 0700–0800

SUSANNA IN VISION
Good morning Britain – coming up on the show.

The Manifestos keep on coming. Today UKIP promise more money for defence and a return to smoking in pubs.

PIERS
CLEGG OPEN ULAY

While the Lib Dems say they'll give more money to the NHS and Education.

SUSANNA
GUN LAWS OPEN ULAY

Guns for his little girl. We'll meet the father of a ten year old who owns NINE guns.

PIERS
BARLOW OPEN ULAY

Swapping the boyband for Broadway. Gary Barlow tells us why he owes his stage success to James Corden.

ANIMATE DATE GRAPHIC / TAKE TITLES + INCLUDING VOICEOVER

SUSANNA
Now though here's Kate with this morning's top story.

SUSANNA
We know that using a mobile phone while driving makes us more likely to have an accident and yet many of us still do it.

SHAUN STILL ULAY

Shaun Worthington died on his way home from a speed awareness course when he crashed into a lorry. An inquest into his death yesterday heard that he had sent a text message just seconds before the accident.

DX LEEDS
We'll be talking to Shaun's family in a moment. But first,

SUSANNA IN VISION

Nick Dixon on just how dangerous using a phone at the wheel can be.

TEXTING AT THE WHEEL VT

SUSANNA
Shaun's mum Jane and his step-dad John join us from their home in Leeds.

PIERS
Describe for us what happened on the day of the crash? Shaun had been on a driving awareness course?

DX LEEDS

Was Shaun normally a safe driver?

Why do you want to warn other drivers from making the same mistake as Shaun?

What was Shaun like and what will you miss most about him?

SUSANNA
TIMECHECK

Coming up,

Rapper Drake reveals how it felt to kiss Madonna. Andi has the details…

DRAKE MADONNA TEASE ULAY

Artist:TAKE THAT

GRAMS:SHINE – TAKE THAT IN @ 55

DX7 ROOF

SUSANNA OOV
Many of you are waking up to glorious sunshine, for those of you not seeing it yet, don't worry – in 5 minutes, Laura will have news of the heat wave rising up the country.

PIERS
He's sold more than 50 million records in the UK and had sell-out tours all over Europe but Take That's Gary Barlow has yet to crack America.

SUSANNA
But that could all be about to change with a musical about Peter Pan. Ross King, our own boy who's never grown up is in New York. Ross, Barlow's about to hit Broadway then…
DX8 NEW YORK

ROSS PICKS UP
- Yes well I'm up and wide awake in the hustle and bustle of New York City where I've been catching up with Gary Barlow who has penned the songs for new Broadway musical, Finding Neverland.

- As the title suggests, the production was inspired by the Oscar winning film of the same name and tells the story of how Peter Pan was written by author J.M. Barrie and who provided inspiration for the well known tale.

- I hit the streets of the Big Apple to find out more with this exclusive chat with the star…

ROSS THROWS TO VT

GARY BARLOW GMB VT

SUSANNA
Competition time now – here's another chance for you to win a huge £60,000.

SINGLE COMP GMB WED B VT

PIERS
Laura's in Cambridgeshire this morning with the weather. Morning Laura.

LAURA
WEATHER SCRIPT

LAURA
Here's a summary for you…

WEATHER SUMMARY

THIS IS ON THE SOFA WITH JUST SUSANNA & PIERS

SUSANNA
You're watching Good Morning Britain – coming up

FROZEN FANS TEASE ULAY

It's the Disney film that made 900 million at the box office and even dominated the charts…

(PAUSE)

CUE SUSANNA OOV

Andi Peters is here to tell us how Frozen became more popular than Taylor Swift.

PIERS

CELEB TEASE ULAY

And his friends include the likes of Tom Cruise, George Clooney and Jennifer Aniston. We'll be joined by the Russian Billionaire Aleksandr the Meerkat.

SUSANNA

That's all still to come but now at TIMECHECK here's Kate with this morning's top story.

KATE

Those are this morning's top stories – back to Susanna and Piers.

PIERS

Coming up,

GUN TEASE ULAY (ulay is mute)

After a series of recent shootings in America, we speak to a father who tells us why he trusts his 10 year old with guns and why the laws cannot punish people before crimes are committed.

BREAK

13

REALITY TV SHOWS

Reality television is an unscripted genre that follows a group of characters or celebrities in a given situation. This can be studio-based, such as *Big Brother*, or can be more of an observational documentary shot on location, like *Keeping up with the Kardashians*. For the purpose of this book we will be looking more closely at studio reality television and how you create this style of show in a studio environment.

Reality as it is known today really exploded on our screens in the late 1990s with the introduction of such global formats as *Survivor* (battling it out to be the last one standing on a desert island) and *Big Brother* (described as a social experiment where participants try and avoid being voted off by their peers). These types of formats, often competition-based, had the added drama of the elimination that had not been seen in this form before, where the viewer at home could affect the show's outcome and the characters' fate by an interactive vote. Reality TV voting also gives viewers a sense of ownership and creates 'water-cooler moments' as audiences become engaged and enraged by what is happening on the show.

Reality television has faced some criticism, mostly focusing on the use of the word 'reality', with critics arguing that these shows put contributors in artificial situations and people are not really acting like themselves. Also, some feel it creates a whole new raft of people famous for being famous, but these shows have also discovered some strong talent that have gone on to have successful television careers.

In this chapter we will concentrate on the daddy of all reality studio formats, *Big Brother*, and explore how all the drama and showdowns are created on a set in Borehamwood at Elstree Studios.

History of the Studio Reality Format

During the 1960s programmes began showing ordinary people, in ordinary situations, screened for our viewing entertainment. This usually took the form of fly-on-the-wall documentaries such as ITV's *Seven Up* (1964), which broadcast interviews with 12 seven-year-olds from a variety of backgrounds about their everyday lives, and was to be updated every seven years. Other early forerunners of reality TV were *The Newlywed Game*, which tested how well newly married couples knew each other, and *The Gong Show*, an amateur talent contest, which both featured contributors eager to do whatever they had to in the name of a TV competition.

In the 1980s it became more commonplace to use videotape over film. Later, the introduction of non-linear post-production software such as Avid meant that more material could be filmed and then crafted into storylines during the edit process, and this changed the way development teams started to think about new ideas. Nigel Duthie, Avid editor for reality shows such as *X Factor The Winner's Story*, *Strictly Come Dancing It Takes Two*, and *The Boss is Coming to Dinner* says:

> Avid made it possible to deal with hours of footage, which had previously been a time-consuming process – not to mention expensive! Hours and hours of material are generated on reality shows. Some literally film 24 hours a day. You are looking for those sparks and moments in the edit to shape into storylines. A lot of the drama that reality television has is built in post-production. Fast cutting [and] dramatic music add to the tension and excitement for the viewer.

The first pre-cursor to *Big Brother* and the style of studio reality that we know today was the series *Number 28*, which aired on Dutch television in 1991. This was where the idea of putting strangers together and seeing how they react first began. The series helped develop many of the conventions and format points that have become synonymous with reality TV. This concept was seen again a year later with the success of MTV's *The Real World*. This led to an explosion of reality TV formats and the elimination formula was born. Most notable were the *Big Brother* (studio-based) and the *Survivor* (location-based) franchises which really captured the public's imagination. These formats really developed the possibilities of interactivity, with public votes, live streaming and online forums.

2012 onwards has seen a move away from studio reality and an increase in reality formats shot in 'real life' situations on location such as *The Only Way is Essex* and *Made in Chelsea,* which both follow the glamorous people of the area in an observational documentary style. These shows try to mimic the appearance and structure of soap opera, with plenty of drama and cliffhangers. Often these formats focus on relationships and entanglements between the on-screen talent. Compelling television is the name of the game and both the production team and cast ensure the camera is rolling at the most dramatic moments. Celebrity versions following celebrities about their daily activity are big business: *The Osbournes, Keeping Up with the Kardashians* and *The Anna Nicole Show* were all international hits.

Key Ingredients

Reality TV often constructs reality, placing contributors into situations which they might otherwise not enter and seeing how they react and interact with their fellow cast members. In competition-based reality shows such as *Big Brother,* there is often the added jeopardy of the elimination round to try and survive. In many reality shows, the camera style and editing gives the viewer the sense that they are passive observers following people going about their daily tasks and activities. Rebecca Yang, CEO of IPCN, distributor of *The Voice of China* and *China's Got Talent* and executive producer of *China's Next Top Model,* talks about top ingredients for a successful reality format:

> One is obviously a good cast. That is very important because the people make the show, whether it is the celebrity that we bring on board or whether it is the contestants that we choose. The second is choosing the right platform. I think choosing the right channel is important in China because it is such a fragmented market; so what makes people in the North smile will not necessarily communicate to people in the South, so a dancing show never works in Beijing, but it works in the East. Cantonese people don't even watch Mandarin talent shows, they will just see some shows from Hong Kong, so it's important the channel matches your demographic. Thirdly promotion. It is such a big country, you really have to shout and that is probably where some lessons were learned from our previous show, Secret Millionaire. The ratings weren't as big as expected but the show itself, honestly speaking, was very well produced. We believe

if the show has good people it will attract an audience, but that is not necessarily the case in China because it is just too big. You really have to shout about it.

In producing reality shows, common key considerations are:

▸ Larger-than-life cast;
▸ The studio set;
▸ The vote/elimination;
▸ The challenges/situations to place them in;
▸ The winner/what is at stake?

Larger-than-life cast and talent are important factors. The viewer needs to connect with the characters and engage with their antics over the coming episodes/weeks. Kate Broadhurst, series producer for ITV's *Judge Rinder* says:

> The choice of talent within a studio format is absolutely vital for the success of a show. Specifically for this show it was particularly important. Although we (as a production team) have always wanted to make a court show in Britain we knew it would only work with the correct judge. It was important that the show had iconography that was recognisable and immediately resonated with the audience, the most important of which was the Judge himself. We always believed that a central 'character' was essential to give the court credence, interest and continuity. This is the first factual court show which has been a success on British TV and one of only a few daytime shows which was launched with an eponymous title to a complete unknown talent. It was a conscious decision and we never questioned why anyone would watch a show with an unknown judge even though it was a risk. It was more important to have the judge central to the action and be the focal point of the show – this should give an insight into how important the talent of a studio show is (that's not to say that the content isn't just as important but a good host/judge/talent will ensure that whatever the content, the most is produced from it).
>
> In this case the show was built around Robert. He had met a commissioner and from there she suggested a meeting between him and the exec; we took him out for lunch to decide if we could make a show and knew within ten minutes that we could and what that show would be. He had the correct personality, presence, gravitas, humour and was also authentic and well-respected and renowned as a criminal barrister.

The studio set is where the action takes place. In *Big Brother* the interior of the set changes year-on-year and generally reflects a new twist in the game. As the series has progressed there have been stricter rules and consequences, and the set has featured a harsher colour scheme and a more claustrophobic setting which seems to encourage more dramatic behaviour. In the third series the set was devised to create a house of two halves – rich and poor. A row of bars divided the housemates. In every series there has been a garden, which includes a jacuzzi and sometimes other luxuries.

In *Judge Rinder* the courtroom is constructed in the studio. Shooting in the studio gives much more control than being in a real working courtroom, which would mean working around the court schedule. It also means cameras and lights can be easily positioned with the set allowing for all the space needed for a crew to be able to move. Kate Broadhurst says:

> US court shows, in particular *Judge Judy*, are shot downwards. We shoot with our cameras at eye level, again to enhance the storytelling and to help the audience feel included within the action rather than watching it as a detached observer. The public gallery in the *Judge Rinder* studio courtroom is occupied by real members of the public rather than paid actors/extras. This also helps with an authentic feel and elicits a real-life reaction to the cases, adding to the atmosphere in the studio.

Contributors generally are filmed competing to win a prize, often while living together in a confined space. The confined space and the pressure to win adds to conflict – a classic reality television ingredient. Voting is either at the hands of the fellow contributors, a panel of judges, or the TV voting public. Endemol's *Big Brother* was hugely innovative in this genre. The iconic 'diary room chair' allowed contestants to go and vent their frustrations to an anonymous voice (*Big Brother*) like a confessional box. This is also where they would nominate their fellow housemates for eviction. Over the years *Big Brother* has played with this, adding to house tension by playing back to fellow housemates what has been said about them. Many reality shows have developed this further by setting challenges to see how characters will react. *Next Top Model* and *I'm a Celebrity… Get Me Out Of Here* both use this device.

Where winning a cash prize is at stake, like in *Big Brother*, during their time in the house the housemates are given tasks to perform which could impact their shopping budget or other privileges within the house. Another studio reality game show was *Shattered*, which set out to see if a group of people could stay awake for a week! They were put in a house (studio) and given tasks, and the jackpot of £100,000 was reduced whenever someone was caught sleeping. This led to formats such as *24 Hours With a Celebrity*, all shot in a studio on a purpose-built set. In the case of reality shows where the prize is a real job (a modelling contract in *Next Top Model*, a record contract in *Idol*, a chef in *MasterChef*), the show revolves around a skill that contributors would have been pre-screened for. They would then have to perform tasks based on their competence in that skill and would be kept or removed at the mercy of a panel of experts or one single expert. A sub-genre of this style is musicals. In this case the winner would win a role in a musical, show, or film, such as *The Glee Project, Any Dream Will Do* and *How Do You Solve A Problem Like Maria?*

Next Top Model is an interesting example of combining studio sets with filmed VT inserts to tell the journey the wannabe models take in their quest to win a modelling contract. Rebecca Yang says:

> In the UK Britain's Next Top Model is unlike China's version: We have made it into a much more grand and positive life-changing reality show. So it is about finding the beauty that represents China. In China it is not about the host, it is about the models, it is their show. So we have changed that into a sort of, the destiny is in your hands, it is your show, it is your journey. Secondly, all the challenges in the show, all the photo shoots, these are completely tailored to the appreciation of the Chinese audience and also the storytelling; we have five Chinese scriptwriters writing the whole thing as it is more scripted reality. We will tell the story, for example, about a single-parent family girl from northern China and all she wants to do is give her mother a flat, a house, so we are trying to tap into what the Chinese people want from an inspiring journey.

Reality shows have the power to instantly transform normal members of the public into celebrities, even if the status is short-lived. Most notably this occurs in talent show reality formats which have created many stars, some with more longevity than others. Often the winners of these formats exploit their status with fame in media, merchandising avenues, even writing autobiographies of their experiences. While they may be famous for being famous, and regarded as the lower-ranking celebrities, some have gone on to achieve genuine success – the brand that is Kim Kardashian is the most notorious reality star, worth millions.

Case Study: *Big Brother*

Big Brother is a huge international reality game show television franchise, created by producer John de Mol in 1997. The format follows a selection of contributors known as 'housemates' who are living together in an isolated environment in a 'studio' house with cameras following their every move. Every week, housemates nominate each other, with those gaining the most votes facing the public vote. The aim is to avoid being nominated and avoid elimination. The series premiered on Channel 4 on 18 July 2000 and was a hit. There was a 24-hour live feed so fans could view inside the house day or night. *Big Brother* aired for 11 series on Channel 4 until it moved to Channel 5 in August 2011.

Behind the Scenes with *Big Brother*'s Former Series Editor David Williams

David Williams is the BBC Creative Director of Entertainment North. He worked his way up through the ranks of *Big Brother* from assistant producer to series editor.

What was your role on *Big Brother*?

I came completely at the right time to benefit from these great huge juggernaut shows. They do allow you, when they are returning shows, to work your way up the ranks. So I started off as an assistant producer on the live show on the live team and I was the series editor by the end. I looked after it from Channel 4's side as their commissioning editor as well.

How was it commissioned?

It was commissioned off the back of the Dutch version, which was the first territory that it came out of. It was packaged in a different way, it sold itself as a social experiment, and the term of reality television was really coined. At Channel 4 they did keep a sense that this was television that was telling you something about people and society more broadly. But it was seen as an experiment, as a social experiment, and therefore gained attraction in quite a few different ways. It was quite a different shape for people to watch stripped across the week, with nightly shows reflecting what had happened the previous day. So it was bold, technically and operationally – perfect for Channel 4 where its remit was to be innovative.

Image 13 *Big Brother* bedroom (Courtesy of Endemol UK)

How would you sum up the format?

The format undoubtedly plays into our voyeuristic tendencies to spy on a group of people. In the mix there is somebody perhaps that echoes some of your thoughts or experiences that you can relate to. The characters are thrust together with people who they would ordinarily not meet, so it is all about the human condition, it's all about competition. I think the genius of *Big Brother* is the nomination element, which is now a factor in so many shows, the whittling down, the competition, just being hardwired in a constant paranoia so people can never quite relax because they are being continually judged. That is the genius of *Big Brother*.

How does the schedule run?

The schedule of *Big Brother* had not been done before in the UK, that a non-scripted programme would place seven days a week for week after week. It obviously grew and it was initially seven weeks. But that was still a massive shakeup and it was not many channels that would devote an hour of their peak-time daily schedule for weeks on end to a new programme – it was a massive risk. If one week into the programming it hadn't worked, I don't know what would have happened. I think they probably would have just ridden it out but it would have been terrible, you know. It would have impacted enormously [on] that channel's performance for the year had it bombed.

Tell us about the production team – the crew that makes the programme
The smartest element of *Big Brother* in all senses from the format to the scheduling actually, I believe, was the organisation that went into generating that much content so quickly with the turnaround and of such quality. It is an organisational tour de force that programme, and that model has now been copied. It was perfected in this country and is now being copied in that strict model and it is based on teamwork. It can't be anything other than a team effort because of the 24-hour nature of it. It is ultimately a live show for weeks on end and so it forces a discipline on everyone involved, that they are a small but vital piece of the machine, but actually your ability to communicate your part of the process to the next person and to be able to follow a brief is the only thing that works. It has to be joined up and that communication is where it lives or dies and is brilliant.

What about the casting?
The casting, we had some years where much as we tried as producers with ideas, with format beats to liven it up, it just didn't work. Once the casting was set, once the dye is cast and the people are sent into the house, if for whatever reason they are not engaging, don't gel, rub each other up the wrong way, if they don't provide interesting watching just as they are, everything else is really small detail. It lives or dies by the strength of the casting – that of course is at the heart of pretty much every contributor non-scripted programme. These have got to be people: you don't have to love them, but you have to engage and they have to be watchable.

How hard is it to incorporate diverse talents?
Again, going back to its roots, in a programme like *Big Brother*, where it was about society throwing a mirror up to the UK at whichever year it was, it was only ever going to be a diverse cast and it was about putting people together who wouldn't perhaps ordinarily meet. That was very much an ethos of *Big Brother* but now it is just a given, and rightly so, that on-screen there should be people that represent the breadth of the audience watching and equally the people behind the cameras have to equally be able to represent and come from their perspective, as opposed to it being made by people for a certain sub-section of society.

What is the future of the format?
I think the production team are very smartly invigorating it and have tweaked the format for its new home where again it serves a slightly different audience. The genius of that format is it can reflect, it has

that ability. It has that ability to be able to be perfected and tweaked for the audience to which it is meant rather than other more rigid formats.

Summary

▸ Casting is key. Without engaging characters even the best format will fail.
▸ The set can act as the construct. Once you put your characters into the house (if it's *Big Brother*) or the kitchen (for *MasterChef*) see how they react and what happens.
▸ The studio and the format provide control over this style of reality more so than observational documentary reality.
▸ The elimination/the public vote gave a fresh edge to this format – this adds excitement for the viewer who feels a sense of ownership over the format. Interactivity remains key to building audiences for these shows – with characters from reality attracting millions of followers on social media.
▸ Reality shows both in the studio and on location can act as a mirror on society and reflect a slice of life.

Insider Knowledge

Never underestimate how long casting takes for these kinds of shows. Usually executive producers and channel commissioning editors will want to sign off on each of the characters you are proposing to use. Backups for the backups will be needed to ensure your show is ready for launch night. Students often find casting for shows difficult and are surprised when people drop out the night before filming. Make sure this does not happen to you. Have a plan B and think about how you can entice your contributors and ensure they all arrive in good time for your record.

Now Try This

1. Practise your own version of *Big Brother* with the script sample attached.
2. Create character biographies for ten contestants. Who would be your ideal cast? What kind of jobs would they have? What would be their likes/dislikes? Would you cast polar opposites?
3. Now come up with your own style of studio reality show. Think about the set as a starting point. Are you going to stage it in a house, a jail, a kitchen or something brand-new? What will the winner get? What is the motivation for taking part? What kind of journey will your contestants be on – is it about personal growth or to learn a new skill like cooking? If stuck for ideas think of your favourite show and try building an elimination format around it. What would that look like?

Sample Script: *Big Brother Live* Eviction

(4. ON VIZ ON SCREEN)

CAM 1: JIB + AQ
CAM 2: HEAD ON PODS
TRIPOD SPOT TOWER/ H/H /
TRIPOD ORBIT
CAM 3: 86:1
CAM 4: WA + TRACK
CAM 5: H/H /TRIPOD +
ROLLOING BASE + AQ
CAM 6: TRIPOD / H/H
HENMAN HILL/TRACK +
OSPREY + AQ
CAM 7: WA + TRACK
CAM 8: TRIPOD ORBIT

14 X 9 PROTECTED
16 X 9 ANAMORPHIC

BIG BROTHER (SUMMER 2015)

TX 9: 9TH LIVE EVICTION

FRIDAY 26TH JUNE, 2015

LIVE THROUGHOUT

SEQ 1. <u>EVS A: PRE-TITLES TEASE</u>
<u>(0'45")</u>

5. **EVS A**

PRE-TITLES

IN:

DUR:

SEQ 1. <u>EVS C: BB OPENING TITLES</u>
<u>(0'17")</u>

SOEVS C
ONLY

6. **EVS C**

OPENING TITLES
C = FILL
D = MATTE

IN:

OUT: MUSIC END

DUR: 0'17"

APPLAUSE

(6 NEXT)

(6. ON EVS C, Scene 2)

1,2,3,4,5,6,STREAM
A,VIZ

SEQ 3.HELLO & WELCOME /
SOLICITY VOTING NUMBERS X 8
LINK TO VT: REALITY PART 1
(4'30)

7. **6**　　　　　　　　**CROWD CHEERING**

BWS SET, SMALL Z/I

MARCUS V/O:
Please welcome your host ....

8. **1**

HA WS DEV TO EYE

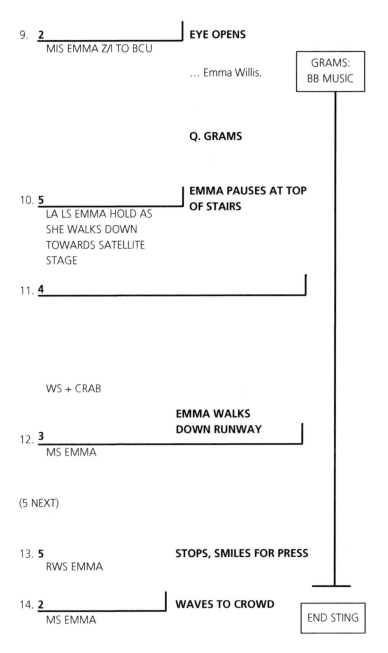

9. **2** — EYE OPENS
MIS EMMA Z/I TO BCU

… Emma Willis.

GRAMS:
BB MUSIC

Q. GRAMS

10. **5** — EMMA PAUSES AT TOP OF STAIRS
LA LS EMMA HOLD AS
SHE WALKS DOWN
TOWARDS SATELLITE
STAGE

11. **4**

WS + CRAB

**EMMA WALKS
DOWN RUNWAY**

12. **3**
MS EMMA

(5 NEXT)

13. **5** — STOPS, SMILES FOR PRESS
RWS EMMA

14. **2** — WAVES TO CROWD
MS EMMA

END STING

15. **3** ⌐
        AUDIENCE

                                    EMMA ON SATELLITE

| ON LED SCREEN: |
| REALITY ON STREAM A1 |

16. **1** ⌐   **EMMA:**
        WS DEV TO MS
        EMMA + SCREEN   Hello and welcome to Big Brother
                                    Time Bomb LIVE and our NINTH
                                    live eviction.

17. **5** ⌐   **CHEERS**
        GS CHEERS

18. **1** _____⌐
        A/B

                                    It's been a week of rivalries, rebellion, and
                                    Ready Brek rage but it wasn't just Nikki
                                    who had her nose knocked out of joint …

19.   **VIZ** _____   **#BBUK**
        #BBUK
        (WHEN SHOT HAS
        SETTLED)

(EVS B NEXT)

(19. ON VIZ, Scene 3)

20.   **EVS B** _____⌐   All week Helen has been driving Brian up
        HOUSE H'LIGHTS   the wall, but on Tuesday night he made a
        ULAY IN SCREEN   dramatic jump over it.

                                    And with Brian doing one, Helen thought
                                    Christmas had come early… until it
                                    actually did. But boy did Santa deliver the
                                    goods with Aisleyne making a sensational
                                    return to the house.

It looks like Helen may have met her match – but luckily for her, we're blowing the whistle tonight as she and Nikki leave the house for good.

But they're not the only ones packing their bags... tonight **CRISTIAN, DANNY, HARRY, JACK, JOEL, NICK, SAM AND SIMON** all face the public vote.

> ANIMATE SCREEN
> TO STREAM A1

Our magic eight have well and truly been shaken by tag nominations but the only question that they want answered is "who'll be leaving tonight?"
Remember – you're voting to EVICT.

> GRAMS:
> BB BED

REALITY FF

21. **STREAM A**
     FF REALITY

(VIZ NEXT)

---

21. ON STREAM A, Scene 3)

22. **VIZ**

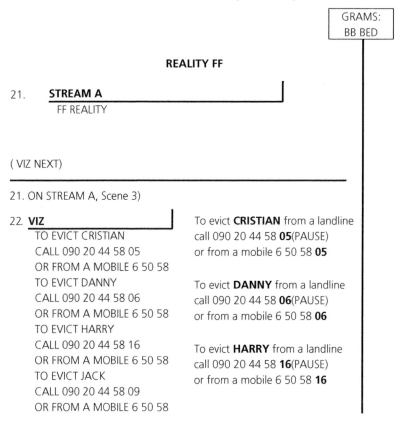

TO EVICT CRISTIAN
CALL 090 20 44 58 05
OR FROM A MOBILE 6 50 58
TO EVICT DANNY
CALL 090 20 44 58 06
OR FROM A MOBILE 6 50 58
TO EVICT HARRY
CALL 090 20 44 58 16
OR FROM A MOBILE 6 50 58
TO EVICT JACK
CALL 090 20 44 58 09
OR FROM A MOBILE 6 50 58

To evict **CRISTIAN** from a landline
call 090 20 44 58 **05**(PAUSE)
or from a mobile 6 50 58 **05**

To evict **DANNY** from a landline
call 090 20 44 58 **06**(PAUSE)
or from a mobile 6 50 58 **06**

To evict **HARRY** from a landline
call 090 20 44 58 **16**(PAUSE)
or from a mobile 6 50 58 **16**

To evict **JACK** from a landline
call 090 20 44 58 **09**(PAUSE)
or from a mobile 6 50 58 **09**

22. **VIZ**
    TO EVICT JOEL
    CALL 090 20 44 58 11
    OR FROM A MOBILE 6 50 58
    TO EVICT NICK
    CALL 090 20 44 58 13
    OR FROM A MOBILE 6 50 58
    TO EVICT SAM
    CALL 090 20 44 58 18
    OR FROM A MOBILE 6 50 58
    TO EVICT SIMON
    CALL 090 20 44 58 15

To evict **JOEL** from a landline
call 090 20 44 58 **11**(PAUSE)
or from a mobile 6 50 58 **11**

To evict **NICK** from a landline
call 090 20 44 58 **13**(PAUSE)
or from a mobile 6 50 58 **13**

    OR FROM A MOBILE 6 50

(STREAM A NEXT)

(23. ON VIZ, Scene 3)

To evict **SAM** from a landline
call 090 20 44 58 **18**(PAUSE)
or from a mobile 6 50 58 **18**

To evict **SIMON** from a landline
call 090 20 44 58 **15**(PAUSE)
or from a mobile 6 50 58 **15**

24. **STREAM A**
    STAY WITH
    FF REALITY

Here's Marcus.

MARCUS V/O:
Mobile and BT landline votes cost
50p. Other landlines may vary. Or
you can vote via the Big Brother
app, where two votes will cost you
99p. Voting closes in tonight's
show. Votes cast after lines
close won't count. Please
don't try to vote if you're
watching on catchup or
outside the UK.

GRAMS:
MARCUS
NO WEB

25. **5**

	EMMA BACK IN VISION:
HOLD EMMA FROM SAT. TOWARDS IRIS, INCL. SCREEN	You can find terms on the Big Brother website. (WALK)

26. **VIZ**

VIZ: bigbrother.channel5.com/terms

bigbrother.channel5.com/
terms

**EMMA ON SATELLITE
WALK TOWARDS IRIS**

(5 NEXT)

14

IT'S A WRAP!

We have taken you through a whistle-stop tour of some of the main studio genres and key ingredients to consider which will help you make successful studio productions. There are many instances of overlap between genres and many things apply to all good studio programmes, so remember the S.T.U.D.I.O. acronym:

S – Set up

Timing is everything and you have to keep to a tight schedule. Time is money in the studio.

T – Talent

Casting is crucial – you need engaging characters and great actors and presenters to make your show pop.

U – Unity

Unity is strength in the studio environment. Build a good team with a strong work ethic and make sure everyone knows what their roles and responsibilities are.

D – Director

The director is the kingpin in making everything come together. They must have strong communication skills to get the best out of cast and crew and of course, visual flair.

I – Innovation

Find the next big thing. Be creative. You need a great idea and script that actors and contributors want to be on, commissioners are excited by and viewers will watch!

O – Obstacles

You need to be a troubleshooter – stay ahead of the game and always have a plan B and C!

The best advice we ever received at the start of our careers is if it's fun to make and something you would like to watch, then you are halfway there. Studio shows require lots of preparation and often involve large crews and production personnel, all with a key role to play. The more preparation you do, the more chance of success you have.

The programmes and films you make at university or college and in your spare time, give you real first-hand experience of just what it takes to make it in the industry. These also act as a calling card when you are trying to get interviews and break into the media world. You need to give yourself an edge over your peers who are all competing for the same jobs as you. If you have managed to secure a famous presenter for your show or devised an exciting social media campaign, this will help you stand out.

For this book we have interviewed TV execs, producers and directors in the UK, USA, Australia and China. Here are some of their top tips on how to break in to the industry.

David Williams, BBC Creative Director of Entertainment North

You need to love television. I was going to come out with something about being tenacious actually, and of course you have to be, to get your foot in the door, but what I have found time and time again with people starting out now is they don't watch a great deal of television. An awful lot, especially in developing ideas, is knowing what has been before.

Maddy Darrall, Co-Founder of Darrall Macqueen and Executive Producer of *Teletubbies*

If you are going in at a junior level on a studio production, never stop watching and listening to what everyone else is doing. Everyone else will assume that you will know what to do, when not to drink coffee, when not to speak – watch and learn.

Job Rabkin, Commissioning Editor, *Channel 4 News* Investigations

For news my top tip would be find stories. Find stories that would work on television, watch lots of news on television and see what you like and where you think it fits with the place you want to be. I would say it is an incredibly tough industry. There are a lot of people who want to do it, it is very hard work but it is all about persistence and tenacity and being a bit bold and being a bit cheeky.

Rebecca Yang, CEO of IPCN and Executive Producer of *China's Next Top Model*

I think first of all you have to genuinely have a passion. I think in this industry it is probably what is required the most because it is hard and anybody who gets their hands dirty in production knows it is not easy, it is not glamorous, especially for those people behind the camera.

Graham Sherrington, Director of *Top Gear*, *Grand Designs* and *The F Word*

My top tips for breaking in to the industry are having a real enthusiasm for the industry, watch a lot of TV and start to recognise what is good and what is bad. Most importantly though, decide as early as possible which jobs you want to go into because actually you will then leave university focused on one particular path and develop the skills for that. If you've got the hunger, if you want to keep learning, then actually you are destined to do it. If you are not sure, if you can't really make your mind up, if you think you might want to do something else, then don't do TV!

Werner Walian, Producer of *The Middle* and *The Fresh Prince of Bel-Air*

You have to have patience number one! And I think that that is getting harder and harder because people move up so fast and they want to be that person right away. You have to put that aside and say don't worry about that. Try and get in the door. You want to also stand out from the crowd and your goal is to be the one that stands out. It is not about stabbing someone in the back, but if somebody comes out and says, 'Hey! I need somebody in the...' And before I've even finished my sentence you're saying, 'I'll do it!' You know, those are the people that people will take note of.

Lisa Armstrong, Producer of *Loose Women* and *The Wright Stuff*

The biggest piece of advice that I have taken all along my career is that if you want to do it, if you want to get into being a producer or working in any way in the media, is to get the experience. It's all very well getting the academia side down, but ultimately you also need to make sure that you get the practical side of things.

Martin Scott, Executive Producer of *The Chase*

To break in to the business you need perseverance, patience and to be prepared to start at the bottom. I think people want to start in television at a level where they just are not experienced enough. They feel they are experienced, but they are not, because television is very different to other industries and I think if you are prepared to come in at the bottom and work your way up, you will work your way up very quickly. Be enthusiastic and committed. People have to work hard but if you are prepared to stick it out, you will make it!

Campbell Glennie, Director of Talent Schemes Edinburgh International TV Festival

Chase up every opportunity, go for every coffee. At the end of that coffee, you should always aim to have a couple more names to follow up on. Television has a reputation for being a highly networked industry for better or for worse. Make that work for you – become indispensable and unforgettable and word about you will get around.

Don't be precious about your first roles, as long as you make sure you take something away from everything you do (pick up a new skill, shadow a director, find out what a certain crew member does) – none of it is a waste of time. And be flexible about genre – those at the top of their game have broad experiences that inform what they do now.

Karl Warner, Managing Director, Electric Ray and formerly the youngest ever BBC commissioning editor

Sometimes, moving up the ranks quickly is not the best thing. Learning the job inside out can be invaluable in the long term. Plus my fondest memories of my career have been the earliest parts and I wish I hadn't raced through them. That said, enthusiasm and positivity, offering up new ideas, looking for new inspiration and always smiling will help you win out.

Emily Gale, Head of Talent, FremantleMedia UK

Apply for work experience even if companies can only offer a few days. Don't wait for your final year to do this, start applying as soon as you know you will have free time. What are all those long holidays for, if not for gaining experience of the television industry? When you do get your foot over the threshold, show your gratitude to the team who have welcomed you on to their production. Keep a notebook and pen with you at all times to write down contacts and the invaluable nuggets of wisdom you will be given when you ask for advice. Never be a drain and suck air out of the room – be the radiator, work hard and create warmth and you will go far.

Passion, enthusiasm and commitment will get you noticed. Make as many films and programmes as you can, especially if you are at university or college where you have access to resources. This will help you learn more about the art of television production and your own style as a programme-maker. It will also help develop your creativity. Everyone has their own story of how they made their way into the creative industries but they all share one thing – they never gave up! Go for it!

Glossary

1S/2S/3S   one shot/two shot etc. Refers to the number of people in the camera frame.

Ad lib   often seen in unscripted shows such as talk or panel shows, and refers to unscripted conversation from a guest or contributor.

As directed   requires the camera operators to follow the director's instruction – sometimes also referred to as 'on the fly' shooting.

Aston   refers to on-screen graphic, usually a person's name, location or date. Sometimes referred to as a cap gen (CG), caption generator or a name super, as it is a superimposed image.

BAFTA   British Academy of Film and Television Arts. An independent charity that supports, develops and promotes the moving image. The annual awards ceremony awards excellence across genres.

BARB   Broadcasters' Audience Research Board – the official source of television viewing figures in the UK.

Block-through   rehearsal with talent and cameras to plan scenes and work out which camera will shoot which part of the show, and from which position.

Break bumpers   used either side of an advert break on commercial channels and may be a quiz question or competition. Used by producers to ensure that the audience returns after the ad break.

Cap gen (CG)   see Aston.

CGI   computer-generated imagery-see Aston.

Crab left/right   moving with the camera to the left or right (also known as trunking).

CU	close-up – a shot that on a person would tightly frame their face.
Dolly in/out	moving with the camera forward or backward.
Earpiece	a tiny communication device that the presenter places in their ear so that they can hear the director in the gallery giving instructions.
ECU	extreme close-up. This is a very tight shot of a subject, for example a tight shot of a person's eye, and is used to emphasise a narrative point.
End credits	the list of names and job roles at the end of the programme.
EPG	electronic programme guide.
Establishing shot	a very wide shot that helps to set the scene and put the action in context.
Eye level	on most TV shows the camera is positioned at eye level to the on-screen talent.
Fourth wall	in a soap or sitcom when an actor talks directly to the viewer at home.
Green room	the waiting room for celebrities, actors or guests to use before and after they appear on a show.
Greenlit	idea approved and funding in place.
GV	general view. Required for a VT package. Shots that can be edited in to provide a sense of setting and place.
Handheld	refers to a camera being off a tripod and held by the camera operator.
HD	high definition.
High-angle shot	placing the camera above the action (pointing down).
Intro	introduction to the show or to the guests.
Item	topic or section in a running order.
Jib	Jimmy Jib camera crane means the camera is on a long pole which allows for a sweeping movement.
Link	in a running order or script refers to how the presenter moves from one topic to the next.
Long shot	camera position that includes the whole person in frame.

Low-angle shot	camera positioned close to the ground (looking up at the action/subject).
MCU	medium close-up. A camera shot that on a person covers the head to the chest.
MS	mid shot. A camera shot that on a person includes the head to the waist.
Name super	superimposed image – see Aston.
Ofcom	The Office of Communications. A regulatory body that ensures TV programmes comply with broadcasting standards.
Outro	conclusion of the show when a presenter and guests say their goodbyes.
Over-the-shoulder shot	commonly used in news interviews, it includes part of the interviewee/guest in the shot to provide a sense of the space between them.
Pan left/right	turning the lens to the left or right.
Pedestal (ped) up/down	moving the height of the camera up or down.
Pick-ups	retakes of any additional sequences. On a pre-recorded show, notes are taken of any mistakes, like a presenter fluffing their line or a sitcom not getting laughs, and then these sequences are typically all re-shot at the end of the studio day.
Pre-title tease	the pre-introduction at the start of a talk or magazine show that comes before the title sequence and explains to the audience what is coming up.
PTC	piece-to-camera. When a presenter speaks directly to the camera.
Ready	director calls this to warn the camera operator that they are going to take their shot.
RTS	Royal Television Society, an educational charity promoting the art and science of television. The annual awards ceremony awards excellence across genres.

Running order	provides the overall duration and duration of all segments of a show. This is particularly important for live and as-live shows.
Run-through	fine-tuning rehearsal.
RV	rendezvous. Used on call sheets to signal the meeting time.
RX	recording. Typically seen on the call sheet to indicate the record date for the programme.
Stagger-through	rehearsal that keeps stopping and starting.
Standby	get ready for record. Silence in the studio or on location.
Stings	graphic inserts added into a show.
Strike	pull down the set at end of filming.
Tag line	sometimes referred to as a log line – a single sentence used to describe a programme.
Talkback	communication system used in the studio as a way of the production team relaying information to the studio floor. **Open talkback** is when everyone with access to the talkback system can hear everyone else. **Closed talkback** is used for greater privacy and for the director to talk directly to key people, for example the floor manager or the presenter, through a specific channel.
Tech check	typically takes place at the beginning of a studio day to make sure all the equipment is working.
Tilt up/down	moving the head of the camera up or down.
Titles	programme title sequence.
Tracking shot	where the camera follows the action on a track.
Trail	short for trailer. Used to advertise programmes.
Truck left/right	moving with the camera to the left or right (also known as crabbing).
TX	transmission. The date the show will be on-screen.
Up-sync	in a VT filmed insert this refers to dialogue said in real-time.
USP	unique selling point.
Vlogging	an online video version of a blog.

V/O	Voice-over. The presenter/actor talking over the screen imagery. This is added in the post-production stage to guide the viewer on the content/story.
Vox Pops	vox populi. Latin for 'voice of the people' and commonly included in VTs to give the public a chance to air their opinion.
VT	video tape. Although we are working in a tapeless environment, this term is still used for the film inserts used in magazine and news programmes.
Wipe screen	to get rid of an image on the screen.
Wrap	finished!
WS	wide shot. A shot framed to include the whole person from head to foot.
Zoom in/out	adjust the zoom lens (not the camera) to be closer or further away from the subject.

Notes

1 Michael Michalko, *Thinkertoys: A Handbook of Creative-Thinking Techniques* (New York, 2006)

2 Edward de Bono, *Lateral Thinking: A Textbook of Creativity* (London, 1933)

3 Tony Buzan, *The Mind Map Book: Unlock your Creativity* (Harlow, 2010)

4 Richard Holloway, 'Vernon Kay In Conversation with Richard Holloway', RTS Futures, London, 22 September 2015 (accessed 20 July 2016)

5 Ibid.

6 Ibid.

7 Ibid.

8 Ibid.

9 *Broadcast*, 'Ratings', 27 July 2015

10 *Broadcast*, 'Ratings' 31 August 2015.

11 BARB, 'TV Ownership', available at http://www.barb.co.uk/resources/tv-facts/tv-ownership (accessed 21 September 2015).

Index